I0528499

www.ingramcontent.com/pod-product-compliance
Lightning Source LLC
Chambersburg PA
CBHW051328120626
46547CB00015B/2451

9 781957 109404

מִשְׁלֵי

THE
ISRAEL
BIBLE

PROVERBS

EDITED BY

Rabbi Tuly Weisz

ISRAEL
365

The Israel Bible: Proverbs

First Edition, 2021

The Israel Bible was produced by Israel365 in cooperation with Teach for Israel and is used with permission from Teach for Israel. All rights reserved. The English translation was adapted by Israel365 from the JPS Tanakh. Copyright © 1985 by the Jewish Publication Society. All rights reserved.

Cover image used under license from Shutterstock.com

ISBN 978-1-957109-40-4

A CIP catalogue record for this title is available from the British Library

The Israel Bible: Proverbs is a holy book that contains the name of God and should be treated with respect.

Table of Contents

Introduction

The Hebrew Bible is commonly known as the *Tanakh* which stands for *Torah* (the Five Books of Moses), *Neviim* (the Prophets) and *Ketuvim* (the Writings). The *Tanakh* consists of 24 books that are considered by Jews to be the word of God. While these books have been referred to as the "Old Testament," many Jews reject this label since it implies the replacement of the Hebrew Bible with something newer and prefer the more authentic Jewish name.

The *Tanakh* is not only the most important book known to man, it is God's word that is perfect and absolute. It is therefore a daunting undertaking to publish an edition of the *Tanakh*, and the responsibilities are awesome. There is no room for error or carelessness in dealing with the eternal word of God. Further, upon embarking on such a serious initiative, we ask ourselves if our efforts are gratuitous. Considering the many editions of the Bible in print, is there truly a need for yet another one?

While there are numerous Bibles in circulation today, its most central aspect – the Land of Israel – has often been overlooked. References to Israel appear on nearly every page, and the city of Jerusalem is specifically referred to hundreds of times throughout the Bible. The essential link between Israel and *Torah* is emphasized repeatedly in verses such as, "For instruction (*Torah*) shall come forth from *Tzion*, the word of *Hashem* from *Yerushalayim*" (Micah 4:2).

The miraculous return of the People of Israel to the Land of Israel in our own generation provides the perfect moment for a new volume to fill this void in biblical literature. *The Israel Bible* includes many special features elucidating God's focus on Israel throughout *Tanakh* and there are many additional, multimedia features available on our website **www.theisraelbible.com**.

Ordering and Presentation – In presenting *The Israel Bible*, our goal is to spread awareness of the biblical significance of the Land of Israel as well as the Jewish people's eternal connection to the land, based on the text of the *Tanakh*, the Hebrew Bible. We aim to honor "the God, the People and the Land of Israel" from an Orthodox Jewish perspective. To that end, *The Israel Bible* follows the traditional Jewish ordering of the books and the customary Hebrew division of chapters. Therefore, for example, we count 24 books of *Tanakh* with *Sefer Divrei Hayamim* (Chronicles) appearing last. It is our hope that our rich content will speak to all Jews and non-Jews who appreciate Israel as the God given land of the Jewish people.

English Translation – Throughout history, Jews have studied the Bible in Hebrew, as any form of translation would miss much of the nuance of the original holy tongue in which *Torah* has been transmitted since the days of Moses. However, as many Jews settled in America in the 19th Century, the need for an English translation became necessary. To be sure, there were already English translations prepared over the centuries by Christians, but in the words of the original editors of the Jewish Publication Society (JPS), "The Jew cannot afford to have his Bible translation prepared for him by others. He cannot have it as a gift, even as he cannot borrow his soul from others."

JPS set out in the late 1800s to publish an authoritative English translation "in the spirit of Jewish tradition." It was compiled over decades by some of the leading Jewish scholars of the time. They formed committees and subcommittees to compare existing English versions, considering medieval and modern Jewish commentators. The monumental JPS translation, originally published in 1917, has been updated in recent years, and *The Israel Bible* is proud to utilize the 1984 New Jewish Publication Society (NJPS) version with its modern, clear language, as well as its wide-ranging acceptance as an accurate and high-quality translation. We applied the NJPS translation verbatim, except for a select list of nouns which we replaced with their traditional Hebrew names. This is true even when we found the NJPS translation to be different than the popular translation of a word or phrase and when the NJPS switched the order of the text for the sake of clarity (see, for example, Ezekiel 24:22–24).

Hebrew Transliteration – To give our readers an authentic *Tanakh* experience, every verse that has commentary is transliterated from Hebrew into English. The Hebrew alphabet chart includes our standards for transliteration and pronunciation of Hebrew verses, enabling readers of *The Israel Bible* to decipher key biblical passages in the holy language. Readers can hear the entire Bible read in Hebrew on our website **www.theisraelbible.com**.

There are various standards when it comes to transliterating Hebrew words into English letters. While we have relied primarily on the classical Hebrew transliteration, we have occasionally deviated for the sake of simplicity, clarity and to reflect common usage.

In addition to whole verses, we have also transliterated many proper nouns in the English translation so that our readers can learn the names of key biblical figures and locations in their Hebrew form. As a rule, we chose to transliterate names of people that were central in the establishment and functioning of the nation of Israel, as well as significant places in the Holy Land. Therefore, regarding Adam's sons, for example, only *Shet* (Seth) is transliterated since it was from him that *Noach* (Noah), and ultimately *Avraham* (Abraham), descended. For this reason, there might be verses or sections of *The Israel Bible* that contains multiple names and only some of them are transliterated.

For the same reason, we have transliterated the names of the books of *Tanakh* when referring to them in our introductions and commentary. When referencing a specific chapter or verse, however, we use the English names of the books in our citations for clarity. We also transliterated ideas and concepts that are central to Judaism such as *Shabbat* (Sabbath), the names of the Jewish holidays and the *Beit Hamikdash* (Temple), as well as biblical measurements. Finally, the name of God is transliterated. Out of respect, Orthodox Jews generally refer to the Lord as *Hashem*, which literally means 'the Name.' Referring to God as *Hashem* reminds us that we feel close to Him but also recognize our distance at the same time. To stress this moniker, we transliterated both the Tetragrammaton as well as the name *Elohim* as *Hashem*.

Study Notes – Our unique commentary was compiled by Orthodox Jewish scholars who live in Israel. It is an anthology in the sense that most of the commentary is not original, but draws from traditional teachings of early Jewish Sages and modern rabbinic commentators. We also include quotations from individuals who have played a significant part in the past century of modern Israeli history including Israeli prime ministers, poets and military leaders.

Our commentary can be broken into four categories, three of which are identified by an icon at the beginning of the study note:

 Israel lessons are indicated with an icon bearing the map of Israel and focus on the Land of Israel and the modern State of Israel.

 Jewish lessons are indicated with a *Torah* scroll and teach a concept in Judaism or a classic idea from rabbinic thought.

 Hebrew lessons are represented by an icon bearing the letter *aleph* and focus on the meaning of a Hebrew word or phrase.

All other comments are considered general comments and are not assigned an icon.

Supplemental Material – In addition to our unique translation and original commentary, *The Israel Bible* offers supplementary material to enrich the learning experience of our readers. Before every book of *Tanakh,* we provide an introduction, as well as information, generally in the form of a map, a chart or a list, which is central to the specific book.

Maps – As the purpose of *The Israel Bible* is to highlight the biblical significance of the Land of Israel, significant time was spent researching and preparing maps to bring the physical contours of the holy land to life with great accuracy. However, since there is a lack of information regarding the precise locations of certain ancient cities, some of the places on our maps are approximate or subject to debate. In these cases, we followed the opinion that we are most comfortable with, but acknowledge that there is room for disagreement. We continue to produce new maps, which are available on our website **www.theisraelbible.com/maps**.

Torah Readings – The *Torah* is not just a work that is studied privately, it is also read out loud in synagogue. Every *Shabbat* and holiday a portion of the *Torah* is read, as well as a related section from *Neviim,* the prophets, called the *haftarah.* We included the blessings recited before and after the reading of the *Torah,* a list of the weekly *Torah* portions and their corresponding *haftarot,* and a chart of the *Torah* readings for special days with their corresponding *haftarot.* Readers can always find the current week's *Torah* portion by visiting **www.theisraelbible.com/weekly-torah-portion**. In this volume, we indicate where a new *Torah* portion begins by highlighting the Hebrew verse number with a gray box so readers can follow along with the communal *Torah* readings. Furthermore, we have included prayers for the State of Israel and the soldiers of the Israel Defense Forces (IDF) that are generally recited following the *Torah* reading in synagogue. It is our constant prayer that God watch over the State of Israel and the members of the IDF, who defend Israel every hour of every day.

In 1948, the State of Israel was created providing a modern answer to Isaiah's ancient question, "Is a nation born all at once?" (Isaiah 66:8). *The Israel Bible* was first published in the 70th year of God's miraculous restoration of the People of Israel to the Land of Israel. Jewish wisdom teaches that 70 is a significant number: *Moshe* (Moses) translated the *Torah* into 70 languages for all 70 nations of the world. From our very origins, the Jewish people were meant to be a light unto the 70 nations, spreading God's truth to the masses.

In the seven decades since the modern rebirth of the State of Israel, God's plan has been unfolding with unprecedented speed, dramatic highs and heartbreaking lows. Never has Israel been at the forefront of the world's attention as it is in our generation. Efforts to vilify the Jewish State seem to spread every day across the globe. At the same time, so does the growing movement of millions of non-Jewish biblical Zionists who stand with the nation of Israel as an expression of their commitment to God's word. As we seek to understand the clash of these two conflicting worldviews, the need for *The Israel Bible* has never been so important.

Standing on the great shoulders of those who came before us and emanating from the land that has always served as the birthplace for the Bible, we conclude with a heartfelt prayer: May the Almighty bless our efforts in offering this *Tanakh* to influence the hearts, minds and actions of its readers. In this way, it is our hope to spread God's name so that the publication of *The Israel Bible* brings us one step closer to the final redemption of Israel and the entire world.

Rabbi Tuly Weisz
Editor, *The Israel Bible*

Foreword

The mandate to study God's word daily is interestingly not found in the Five Books of Moses (Pentateuch), but rather in the first book of our prophetic writings: "Let not this Book of the Teaching cease from your lips, but recite it day and night, so that you may observe faithfully all that is written in it. Only then will you prosper in your undertakings and only then will you be successful" (Joshua 1:8). Charged with bringing the Israelites into the land covenantally promised to Abraham, Isaac and Jacob, God ensures Joshua of His protection if the nation observes His ways as dictated in the Divine constitution known as the *Torah*.

In Jewish tradition, Joshua (1:8) is directly linked with Deuteronomy (11:14), "You shall gather in your new grain and wine, and oil."[1] Our Sages deduced from this scriptural combination the importance of merging *Torah* study with a profession. Completely dedicating oneself to the study of *Torah* without having the financial means to sustain this lifestyle can lead one to eventually straying from observance of God's will. Poverty and crime can have an intimate relationship.

We must also be careful that our work does not affect our daily study of Scripture. The addiction of becoming a workaholic and not making *Torah* study a priority can also lead one into temptations that can violate our personal relationship with Him as well as our fellow human beings. The goal is to achieve a healthy balance between our study of God's word and our daily work.

The Deuteronomic verse quoted above is part of the second section of the Shema[2] that discusses the concept of reward and punishment. Sanctifying God by fulfilling His commandments results in the Land of Israel practically benefitting from rains that occur in the right season and reaping the abundance from the fields. However, if the nation follows pagan gods and practices, the consequences are devastating – famine and death. The Land of Israel is intrinsically linked with the keeping of the *Torah*. Covenant Land comes with covenant responsibility.

---

1 Talmud Bavli Berachot 35b

2 Consisting of three sections within the Five Books of Moses (Deut. 6:4–8; 11:13–22 and Numbers 15:37–42), the *Shema* is proclamation of accepting God's Kingdom in our lives, loyalty to His commandments and remembering His redemptive act of liberating us from Egypt. Jews recite the *Shema* twice a day as stated in Deut. 6:7.

Born into slavery, Joshua is now leading His people into the Promised Land. More than 500 years separates him from his ancestral forefather Abraham. The historical narratives that took place between Abraham leaving everything behind to follow God in Genesis 12 and the death of Moses in the last chapter of Deuteronomy are filled with intrigue, suspense, joy, sorrow and hope. What began as a family is now a nation actualizing its mission to be a kingdom of priests to the world. However, for the Israelites to succeed in the Land of Israel, they must see the *Torah* as the only compass to direct their lives.

The biblical episodes after our first entry into the land are well known. Our ancestors' triumphs and sins are all on public record. We learned the harsh reality of Leviticus (18:28) "So let not the land spew you out for defiling it as it spewed out the nation that came before you." Twice, we lost the privilege to be stewards of the Land of Israel and to fulfill our nation state mandate to be a light to the world. However, when the annals of history were ready to archive the Jewish people after the Holocaust, God kept His covenantal promise and gathered us from the four corners of the globe to come home. The year 1948 was a game changer. Biblical prophecies were and are being realized. We are now living in the birth pangs of the messianic era.

In our morning prayers, we recite a series of blessings over the *Torah* that include petitioning God to have a sweet tooth for His word, to study it without any ulterior motive and to have Him to teach it to us. They are some congregations that invoke the following liturgical prayer after the completion of these blessings: *May the Torah be my faith and El Shaddai my help. Blessed be the name of His glorious kingdom forever and all time.*

According to Jewish tradition, the neglect of not blessing the *Torah* before engaging in its study was one of the reasons for the destruction of the Temple.[3] This is deduced from the redundancy of words in Jeremiah (9:12) that talks about Israel not following God: "...Because they forsook the teaching I had set before them. They did not obey Me and they did not follow it [did not make a blessing before studying it]." Our inability to properly cherish God's greatest gift to the world, the *Torah*, led to our eventual exile from our land.

On Israel's Independence Day, Jews around the world recite Psalms 113–118 to express our gratitude to God for His Divine hand in helping establish the State of Israel. We have learned from our past and realize the privilege to see firsthand the land, people and *Torah* operating all together in our generation.

---

3   Babylonian Talmud Nedarim 81a

When Rabbi Tuly Weisz approached me about his intent to publish *The Israel Bible* that would highlight commentary about the special relationship between the land and people, I saw this project as another way to publicly demonstrate our appreciation to God for having the State of Israel. In addition, it is another educational tool to ensure biblical literacy. If we are to truly enjoy the Land of Israel, it is incumbent upon us to continually study the *Torah*. Isaiah once prophesied that the Jewish people would return to Zion with songs, "crowned with everlasting joy" (35:10). *The Israel Bible* provides us the lyrical content to express our joy in living in the land that God calls holy.

Rabbi Shlomo Riskin
Chief Rabbi of Efrat
Founder of the Center for Jewish-Christian
Understanding & Cooperation (CJCUC)

Introduction to Mishlei
The Book of Proverbs

Introduction and commentary by Ahuva Balofsky

The name of this book of wisdom, *Mishlei*, is translated to English as 'Proverbs,' but that is perhaps too limited a designation. The Hebrew word *mashal*, from which the name *Mishlei* is derived, is more akin to an extended metaphor than a pithy saying.

Sefer Mishlei contains the collected wisdom of *Shlomo*, the wisest king to sit on the throne in *Yerushalayim*. In *Melachim* I 3:5–14, the Bible relates how this son of King *David* achieved such greatness. *Hashem* appeared to *Shlomo* in a dream and offered him whatever his heart desired. Young King *Shlomo* asked only for the wisdom to guide God's people in righteousness. So pleased was the Lord with *Shlomo's* request that He granted *Shlomo's* wish and, in addition, also gave him great wealth and success.

Sefer Mishlei refers to the fear of *Hashem* as "the beginning of wisdom" (1:7), noting that recognition of His hand in the world is the source of all understanding. It admonishes the wise to seek out similar companions and to avoid the fool and the temptress, promising reward for the hard-working and dedicated, and suffering for the lazy and the wicked.

On the surface, the lessons of *Sefer Mishlei* seem straightforward, but in his own introduction to the book, King *Shlomo* promises that great secrets lie behind his words. The metaphors in the text can be understood both literally and figuratively, and can be projected onto a number of different situations.

Throughout the text, wisdom is personified as a righteous woman, while temptation is represented by the harlot. King *Shlomo* tells the reader that *Hashem* founded creation itself on wisdom, making order out of the chaos. That wisdom has been understood to be God's *Torah*, and following its precepts will earn the faithful His reward.

Later chapters of *Sefer Mishlei* cite *Agur* son of *Yakeh* and King *Lemuel* as sources for the parables contained within. Jewish tradition considers both to be monikers for King *Shlomo,* as *Agur* means "compiler" and *Lemuel* means "for God".

The final chapter of the book, chapter 31, includes the beautiful passage entitled "A Woman of Valor." This poem, like everything else in *Sefer Mishlei,* can be understood literally, as a description of the ideal woman. However, in Jewish tradition it has been explained as a reference to the matriarch *Sara,* the *Torah* or even the *Shabbat.* In fact, it is customary in many Jewish homes to sing this poem on Friday night around the *Shabbat* table, while welcoming the Sabbath Queen. According to *Metzudat David, Shlomo* chose to end his book of wisdom with a praise of the woman of valor as a tribute to his mother, *Batsheva,* from whom who learned much of the wisdom contained within.

List of Opinions Regarding
When *Shlomo* (Solomon) Authored his Biblical Books

King *Shlomo* authored three of the books of *Tanakh: Mishlei, Shir Hashirim* and *Kohelet.* The first two are attributed to him explicitly (Proverbs 1:1, Song of Songs 1:1). The third is attributed to *Kohelet* son of *David* (Ecclesiastes 1:1) who the Sages tell us was *Shlomo.* There are several possible sequences offered by the Sages regarding the order in which he wrote these books (*Shir Hashirim Rabba* 1:10).

1. *Shlomo* wrote *Mishlei* before *Shir Hashirim* and *Kohelet.* This approach is based on the verse in *Sefer Melachim* I 5:12 which mentions *Shlomo*'s proverbs before his songs.

2. *Shlomo* wrote them all around the same time.

3. *Shlomo* wrote his books following the pattern of human experience. In his youth, when one is more likely to fall passionately in love and write emotional love songs, *Shlomo* authored *Shir Hashirim.* He wrote *Mishlei* as a mature adult when one is most likely to develop parables of wisdom. Finally, *Kohelet* was written in his old age when one is likely to be more serious and somber and to see the vanity in the world.

1 ¹ The proverbs of *Shlomo* son of *David*, king of *Yisrael*:

א מִשְׁלֵי שְׁלֹמֹה בֶן־דָּוִד מֶלֶךְ יִשְׂרָאֵל:

² For learning wisdom and discipline; For understanding words of discernment;

ב לָדַעַת חָכְמָה וּמוּסָר לְהָבִין אִמְרֵי בִינָה:

³ For acquiring the discipline for success, Righteousness, justice, and equity;

ג לָקַחַת מוּסַר הַשְׂכֵּל צֶדֶק וּמִשְׁפָּט וּמֵישָׁרִים:

⁴ For endowing the simple with shrewdness, The young with knowledge and foresight.

ד לָתֵת לִפְתָאיִם עָרְמָה לְנַעַר דַּעַת וּמְזִמָּה:

⁵ The wise man, hearing them, will gain more wisdom; The discerning man will learn to be adroit;

ה יִשְׁמַע חָכָם וְיוֹסֶף לֶקַח וְנָבוֹן תַּחְבֻּלוֹת יִקְנֶה:

⁶ For understanding proverb and epigram, The words of the wise and their riddles.

ו לְהָבִין מָשָׁל וּמְלִיצָה דִּבְרֵי חֲכָמִים וְחִידֹתָם:

⁷ The fear of *Hashem* is the beginning of knowledge; Fools despise wisdom and discipline.

ז יִרְאַת יְהֹוָה רֵאשִׁית דָּעַת חָכְמָה וּמוּסָר אֱוִילִים בָּזוּ:

yir-AT a-do-NAI ray-SHEET DA-at khokh-MAH u-mu-SAR e-vee-LEEM BA-zu

⁸ My son, heed the discipline of your father, And do not forsake the instruction of your mother;

ח שְׁמַע בְּנִי מוּסַר אָבִיךָ וְאַל־תִּטֹּשׁ תּוֹרַת אִמֶּךָ:

⁹ For they are a graceful wreath upon your head, A necklace about your throat.

ט כִּי לִוְיַת חֵן הֵם לְרֹאשֶׁךָ וַעֲנָקִים לְגַרְגְּרֹתֶיךָ:

¹⁰ My son, if sinners entice you, do not yield;

י בְּנִי אִם־יְפַתּוּךָ חַטָּאִים אַל־תֹּבֵא:

¹¹ If they say, "Come with us, Let us set an ambush to shed blood, Let us lie in wait for the innocent (Without cause!)

יא אִם־יֹאמְרוּ לְכָה אִתָּנוּ נֶאֶרְבָה לְדָם נִצְפְּנָה לְנָקִי חִנָּם:

¹² Like Sheol, let us swallow them alive; Whole, like those who go down into the Pit.

יב נִבְלָעֵם כִּשְׁאוֹל חַיִּים וּתְמִימִים כְּיוֹרְדֵי בוֹר:

¹³ We shall obtain every precious treasure; We shall fill our homes with loot.

יג כָּל־הוֹן יָקָר נִמְצָא נְמַלֵּא בָתֵּינוּ שָׁלָל:

¹⁴ Throw in your lot with us; We shall all have a common purse."

יד גּוֹרָלְךָ תַּפִּיל בְּתוֹכֵנוּ כִּיס אֶחָד יִהְיֶה לְכֻלָּנוּ:

¹⁵ My son, do not set out with them; Keep your feet from their path.

טו בְּנִי אַל־תֵּלֵךְ בְּדֶרֶךְ אִתָּם מְנַע רַגְלְךָ מִנְּתִיבָתָם:

¹⁶ For their feet run to evil; They hurry to shed blood.

טז כִּי רַגְלֵיהֶם לָרַע יָרוּצוּ וִימַהֲרוּ לִשְׁפָּךְ־דָּם:

A woman watching the sun rise in the Negev desert

1:7 The fear of *Hashem* is the beginning of knowledge *Sefer Mishlei* contains the collected wisdom of *Shlomo*, the wisest king to sit on the throne in Israel. This verse sets the tone for the entire book of *Mishlei*. Once King *Solomon* has set out his purpose – to impart wisdom – in writing, he begins by identifying fear of *Hashem* as the root of that wisdom. Without awe of God, knowledge is empty and can be twisted for any number of negative purposes.

1

17 In the eyes of every winged creature The outspread net means nothing.

כִּי־חִנָּם מְזֹרָה הָרָשֶׁת בְּעֵינֵי כָל־בַּעַל כָּנָף:

18 But they lie in ambush for their own blood; They lie in wait for their own lives.

וְהֵם לְדָמָם יֶאֱרֹבוּ יִצְפְּנוּ לְנַפְשֹׁתָם:

19 Such is the fate of all who pursue unjust gain; It takes the life of its possessor.

כֵּן אׇרְחוֹת כָּל־בֹּצֵעַ בָּצַע אֶת־נֶפֶשׁ בְּעָלָיו יִקָּח:

20 Wisdom cries aloud in the streets, Raises her voice in the squares.

חׇכְמוֹת בַּחוּץ תָּרֹנָּה בָּרְחֹבוֹת תִּתֵּן קוֹלָהּ:

21 At the head of the busy streets she calls; At the entrance of the gates, in the city, she speaks out:

בְּרֹאשׁ הֹמִיּוֹת תִּקְרָא בְּפִתְחֵי שְׁעָרִים בָּעִיר אֲמָרֶיהָ תֹאמֵר:

22 "How long will you simple ones love simplicity, You scoffers be eager to scoff, You dullards hate knowledge?

עַד־מָתַי פְּתָיִם תְּאֵהֲבוּ פֶתִי וְלֵצִים לָצוֹן חָמְדוּ לָהֶם וּכְסִילִים יִשְׂנְאוּ־דָעַת:

23 You are indifferent to my rebuke; I will now speak my mind to you, And let you know my thoughts.

תָּשׁוּבוּ לְתוֹכַחְתִּי הִנֵּה אַבִּיעָה לָכֶם רוּחִי אוֹדִיעָה דְבָרַי אֶתְכֶם:

24 Since you refused me when I called, And paid no heed when I extended my hand,

יַעַן קָרָאתִי וַתְּמָאֵנוּ נָטִיתִי יָדִי וְאֵין מַקְשִׁיב:

25 You spurned all my advice, And would not hear my rebuke,

וַתִּפְרְעוּ כָל־עֲצָתִי וְתוֹכַחְתִּי לֹא אֲבִיתֶם:

26 I will laugh at your calamity, And mock when terror comes upon you,

גַּם־אֲנִי בְּאֵידְכֶם אֶשְׂחָק אֶלְעַג בְּבֹא פַחְדְּכֶם:

27 When terror comes like a disaster, And calamity arrives like a whirlwind, When trouble and distress come upon you.

בְּבֹא כשאוה [כְשׁוֹאָה] פַּחְדְּכֶם וְאֵידְכֶם כְּסוּפָה יֶאֱתֶה בְּבֹא עֲלֵיכֶם צָרָה וְצוּקָה:

28 Then they shall call me but I will not answer; They shall seek me but not find me.

אָז יִקְרָאֻנְנִי וְלֹא אֶעֱנֶה יְשַׁחֲרֻנְנִי וְלֹא יִמְצָאֻנְנִי:

29 Because they hated knowledge, And did not choose fear of *Hashem*;

תַּחַת כִּי־שָׂנְאוּ דָעַת וְיִרְאַת יְהֹוָה לֹא בָחָרוּ:

30 They refused my advice, And disdained all my rebukes,

לֹא־אָבוּ לַעֲצָתִי נָאֲצוּ כָּל־תּוֹכַחְתִּי:

31 They shall eat the fruit of their ways, And have their fill of their own counsels.

וְיֹאכְלוּ מִפְּרִי דַרְכָּם וּמִמֹּעֲצֹתֵיהֶם יִשְׂבָּעוּ:

32 The tranquillity of the simple will kill them, And the complacency of dullards will destroy them.

כִּי מְשׁוּבַת פְּתָיִם תַּהַרְגֵם וְשַׁלְוַת כְּסִילִים תְּאַבְּדֵם:

33 But he who listens to me will dwell in safety, Untroubled by the terror of misfortune."

וְשֹׁמֵעַ לִי יִשְׁכָּן־בֶּטַח וְשַׁאֲנַן מִפַּחַד רָעָה:

2 1 My son, if you accept my words And treasure up my commandments;

בְּנִי אִם־תִּקַּח אֲמָרָי וּמִצְוֺתַי תִּצְפֹּן אִתָּךְ: **ב** א

2 If you make your ear attentive to wisdom And your mind open to discernment;

לְהַקְשִׁיב לַחָכְמָה אָזְנֶךָ תַּטֶּה לִבְּךָ לַתְּבוּנָה: ב

3 If you call to understanding And cry aloud to discernment,

כִּי אִם לַבִּינָה תִקְרָא לַתְּבוּנָה תִּתֵּן קוֹלֶךָ: ג

4 If you seek it as you do silver And search for it as for treasures,

אִם־תְּבַקְשֶׁנָּה כַכָּסֶף וְכַמַּטְמוֹנִים תַּחְפְּשֶׂנָּה: ד

5 Then you will understand the fear of *Hashem* And attain knowledge of *Hashem*.

אָז תָּבִין יִרְאַת יְהֹוָה וְדַעַת אֱלֹהִים תִּמְצָא: ה

6 For *Hashem* grants wisdom; Knowledge and discernment are by His decree.

כִּי־יְהֹוָה יִתֵּן חָכְמָה מִפִּיו דַּעַת וּתְבוּנָה: ו

7 He reserves ability for the upright And is a shield for those who live blamelessly,

וְצָפֹן [יִצְפֹּן] לַיְשָׁרִים תּוּשִׁיָּה מָגֵן לְהֹלְכֵי תֹם: ז

8 Guarding the paths of justice, Protecting the way of those loyal to Him.

לִנְצֹר אָרְחוֹת מִשְׁפָּט וְדֶרֶךְ חֲסִידֹו [חֲסִידָיו] יִשְׁמֹר: ח

9 You will then understand what is right, just, And equitable – every good course.

אָז תָּבִין צֶדֶק וּמִשְׁפָּט וּמֵישָׁרִים כָּל־מַעְגַּל־טוֹב: ט

10 For wisdom will enter your mind And knowledge will delight you.

כִּי־תָבוֹא חָכְמָה בְלִבֶּךָ וְדַעַת לְנַפְשְׁךָ יִנְעָם: י

11 Foresight will protect you, And discernment will guard you.

מְזִמָּה תִּשְׁמֹר עָלֶיךָ תְּבוּנָה תִנְצְרֶכָּה: יא

12 It will save you from the way of evil men, From men who speak duplicity,

לְהַצִּילְךָ מִדֶּרֶךְ רָע מֵאִישׁ מְדַבֵּר תַּהְפֻּכוֹת: יב

13 Who leave the paths of rectitude To follow the ways of darkness,

הַעֹזְבִים אָרְחוֹת יֹשֶׁר לָלֶכֶת בְּדַרְכֵי־חֹשֶׁךְ: יג

14 Who rejoice in doing evil And exult in the duplicity of evil men,

הַשְּׂמֵחִים לַעֲשׂוֹת רָע יָגִילוּ בְּתַהְפֻּכוֹת רָע: יד

15 Men whose paths are crooked And who are devious in their course.

אֲשֶׁר אָרְחֹתֵיהֶם עִקְּשִׁים וּנְלוֹזִים בְּמַעְגְּלוֹתָם: טו

16 It will save you from the forbidden woman, From the alien woman whose talk is smooth,

לְהַצִּילְךָ מֵאִשָּׁה זָרָה מִנָּכְרִיָּה אֲמָרֶיהָ הֶחֱלִיקָה: טז

17 Who forsakes the companion of her youth And disregards the covenant of her God.

הַעֹזֶבֶת אַלּוּף נְעוּרֶיהָ וְאֶת־בְּרִית אֱלֹהֶיהָ שָׁכֵחָה: יז

18 Her house sinks down to Death, And her course leads to the shades.

כִּי שָׁחָה אֶל־מָוֶת בֵּיתָהּ וְאֶל־רְפָאִים מַעְגְּלֹתֶיהָ: יח

19 All who go to her cannot return And find again the paths of life.

כָּל־בָּאֶיהָ לֹא יְשׁוּבוּן וְלֹא־יַשִּׂיגוּ אָרְחוֹת חַיִּים: יט

20 So follow the way of the good And keep to the paths of the just.

כ לְמַעַן תֵּלֵךְ בְּדֶרֶךְ טוֹבִים וְאָרְחוֹת צַדִּיקִים תִּשְׁמֹר:

21 For the upright will inhabit the earth, The blameless will remain in it.

כא כִּי־יְשָׁרִים יִשְׁכְּנוּ אָרֶץ וּתְמִימִים יִוָּתְרוּ בָהּ:

kee y'-sha-REEM yish-k'-nu A-retz ut-mee-MEEM yi-va-t'-RU VAH

22 While the wicked will vanish from the land And the treacherous will be rooted out of it.

כב וּרְשָׁעִים מֵאֶרֶץ יִכָּרֵתוּ וּבוֹגְדִים יִסְּחוּ מִמֶּנָּה:

3 1 My son, do not forget my teaching, But let your mind retain my commandments;

ג א בְּנִי תּוֹרָתִי אַל־תִּשְׁכָּח וּמִצְוֹתַי יִצֹּר לִבֶּךָ:

2 For they will bestow on you length of days, Years of life and well-being.

ב כִּי אֹרֶךְ יָמִים וּשְׁנוֹת חַיִּים וְשָׁלוֹם יוֹסִיפוּ לָךְ:

3 Let fidelity and steadfastness not leave you; Bind them about your throat, Write them on the tablet of your mind,

ג חֶסֶד וֶאֱמֶת אַל־יַעַזְבֻךָ קָשְׁרֵם עַל־גַּרְגְּרוֹתֶיךָ כָּתְבֵם עַל־לוּחַ לִבֶּךָ:

4 And you will find favor and approbation In the eyes of *Hashem* and man.

ד וּמְצָא־חֵן וְשֵׂכֶל־טוֹב בְּעֵינֵי אֱלֹהִים וְאָדָם:

5 Trust in *Hashem* with all your heart, And do not rely on your own understanding.

ה בְּטַח אֶל־יְהוָה בְּכָל־לִבֶּךָ וְאֶל־בִּינָתְךָ אַל־תִּשָּׁעֵן:

6 In all your ways acknowledge Him, And He will make your paths smooth.

ו בְּכָל־דְּרָכֶיךָ דָעֵהוּ וְהוּא יְיַשֵּׁר אֹרְחֹתֶיךָ:

7 Do not be wise in your own eyes; Fear *Hashem* and shun evil.

ז אַל־תְּהִי חָכָם בְּעֵינֶיךָ יְרָא אֶת־יְהוָה וְסוּר מֵרָע:

8 It will be a cure for your body, A tonic for your bones.

ח רִפְאוּת תְּהִי לְשָׁרֶּךָ וְשִׁקּוּי לְעַצְמוֹתֶיךָ:

9 Honor *Hashem* with your wealth, With the best of all your income,

ט כַּבֵּד אֶת־יְהוָה מֵהוֹנֶךָ וּמֵרֵאשִׁית כָּל־תְּבוּאָתֶךָ:

ka-BAYD et a-do-NAI may-ho-NE-kha u-may-ray-SHEET kol t'-vu-a-TE-kha

10 And your barns will be filled with grain, Your vats will burst with new wine.

י וְיִמָּלְאוּ אֲסָמֶיךָ שָׂבָע וְתִירוֹשׁ יְקָבֶיךָ יִפְרֹצוּ:

 2:21 For the upright will inhabit the earth The word *eretz*, translated here as 'earth,' also means 'land.' According to Yehuda Keel, author of the *Da'at Mikra* commentary on *Sefer Mishlei*, this is a reference to the Land of Israel. In this verse, King *Shlomo* reminds us of *Hashem*'s promise to the Israelites in the desert, that if they walk in His ways, they will remain in the land which He has given them (see Deuteronomy 4:1). *Eretz Yisrael* is promised to those who remain steadfast in their commitment to God's words, not only in deed, but also in thought.

3:9 With the best of all your income *Reisheet kol t'vuatecha* (ראשית כל תבואתך), translated here as 'the best of all your

income,' literally means 'the first of your grain.' Offering the first of our crops to God reminds us how much we owe Him. It is easy to forget how much *Hashem* has given us, as we get caught up in our own efforts towards success. God commands us to bring the first of our harvest each year to the *Beit Hamikdash* in *Yerushalayim* (see Deuteronomy 26:2), to remind us that He is behind everything that happens to us, and the constant source of our success.

The seven species from which the first fruit offering was brought

11 Do not reject the discipline of *Hashem*, my son; Do not abhor His rebuke.

מוּסַר יְהֹוָה בְּנִי אַל־תִּמְאָס וְאַל־תָּקֹץ בְּתוֹכַחְתּוֹ: יא

12 For whom *Hashem* loves, He rebukes, As a father the son whom he favors.

כִּי אֶת אֲשֶׁר יֶאֱהַב יְהֹוָה יוֹכִיחַ וּכְאָב אֶת־בֵּן יִרְצֶה: יב

13 Happy is the man who finds wisdom, The man who attains understanding.

אַשְׁרֵי אָדָם מָצָא חָכְמָה וְאָדָם יָפִיק תְּבוּנָה: יג

14 Her value in trade is better than silver, Her yield, greater than gold.

כִּי טוֹב סַחְרָהּ מִסְּחַר־כָּסֶף וּמֵחָרוּץ תְּבוּאָתָהּ: יד

15 She is more precious than rubies; All of your goods cannot equal her.

יְקָרָה הִיא מִפְּנִיִּים [מִפְּנִינִים] וְכָל־חֲפָצֶיךָ לֹא יִשְׁווּ־בָהּ: טו

16 In her right hand is length of days, In her left, riches and honor.

אֹרֶךְ יָמִים בִּימִינָהּ בִּשְׂמֹאולָהּ עֹשֶׁר וְכָבוֹד: טז

17 Her ways are pleasant ways, And all her paths, peaceful.

דְּרָכֶיהָ דַרְכֵי־נֹעַם וְכָל־נְתִיבוֹתֶיהָ שָׁלוֹם: יז

18 She is a tree of life to those who grasp her, And whoever holds on to her is happy.

עֵץ־חַיִּים הִיא לַמַּחֲזִיקִים בָּהּ וְתֹמְכֶיהָ מְאֻשָּׁר: יח

19 *Hashem* founded the earth by wisdom; He established the heavens by understanding;

יְהֹוָה בְּחָכְמָה יָסַד־אָרֶץ כּוֹנֵן שָׁמַיִם בִּתְבוּנָה: יט

20 By His knowledge the depths burst apart, And the skies distilled dew.

בְּדַעְתּוֹ תְּהוֹמוֹת נִבְקָעוּ וּשְׁחָקִים יִרְעֲפוּ־טָל: כ

21 My son, do not lose sight of them; Hold on to resourcefulness and foresight.

בְּנִי אַל־יָלֻזוּ מֵעֵינֶיךָ נְצֹר תֻּשִׁיָּה וּמְזִמָּה: כא

22 They will give life to your spirit And grace to your throat.

וְיִהְיוּ חַיִּים לְנַפְשֶׁךָ וְחֵן לְגַרְגְּרֹתֶיךָ: כב

23 Then you will go your way safely And not injure your feet.

אָז תֵּלֵךְ לָבֶטַח דַּרְכֶּךָ וְרַגְלְךָ לֹא תִגּוֹף: כג

24 When you lie down you will be unafraid; You will lie down and your sleep will be sweet.

אִם־תִּשְׁכַּב לֹא־תִפְחָד וְשָׁכַבְתָּ וְעָרְבָה שְׁנָתֶךָ: כד

25 You will not fear sudden terror Or the disaster that comes upon the wicked,

אַל־תִּירָא מִפַּחַד פִּתְאֹם וּמִשֹּׁאַת רְשָׁעִים כִּי תָבֹא: כה

26 For *Hashem* will be your trust; He will keep your feet from being caught.

כִּי־יְהֹוָה יִהְיֶה בְכִסְלֶךָ וְשָׁמַר רַגְלְךָ מִלָּכֶד: כו

27 Do not withhold good from one who deserves it When you have the power to do it [for him].

אַל־תִּמְנַע־טוֹב מִבְּעָלָיו בִּהְיוֹת לְאֵל יָדֶיךָ [יָדְךָ] לַעֲשׂוֹת: כז

28 Do not say to your fellow, "Come back again; I'll give it to you tomorrow," when you have it with you.

אַל־תֹּאמַר לְרֵעֶיךָ [לְרֵעֲךָ] לֵךְ וָשׁוּב וּמָחָר אֶתֵּן וְיֵשׁ אִתָּךְ: כח

29 Do not devise harm against your fellow Who lives trustfully with you.

אַל־תַּחֲרֹשׁ עַל־רֵעֲךָ רָעָה וְהוּא־יוֹשֵׁב לָבֶטַח אִתָּךְ: כט

5

30 Do not quarrel with a man for no cause, When he has done you no harm.

ל אַל־תָּרוֹב [תָּרִיב] עִם־אָדָם חִנָּם אִם־לֹא גְמָלְךָ רָעָה׃

31 Do not envy a lawless man, Or choose any of his ways;

לא אַל־תְּקַנֵּא בְּאִישׁ חָמָס וְאַל־תִּבְחַר בְּכָל־דְּרָכָיו׃

32 For the devious man is an abomination to *Hashem*, But He is intimate with the straightforward.

לב כִּי תוֹעֲבַת יְהוָה נָלוֹז וְאֶת־יְשָׁרִים סוֹדוֹ׃

33 The curse of *Hashem* is on the house of the wicked, But He blesses the abode of the righteous.

לג מְאֵרַת יְהוָה בְּבֵית רָשָׁע וּנְוֵה צַדִּיקִים יְבָרֵךְ׃

34 At scoffers He scoffs, But to the lowly He shows grace.

לד אִם־לַלֵּצִים הוּא־יָלִיץ וְלַעֲנִיִּים [וְלַעֲנָוִים] יִתֶּן־חֵן׃

35 The wise shall obtain honor, But dullards get disgrace as their portion.

לה כָּבוֹד חֲכָמִים יִנְחָלוּ וּכְסִילִים מֵרִים קָלוֹן׃

4 1 Sons, heed the discipline of a father; Listen and learn discernment,

ד א שִׁמְעוּ בָנִים מוּסַר אָב וְהַקְשִׁיבוּ לָדַעַת בִּינָה׃

2 For I give you good instruction; Do not forsake my teaching.

ב כִּי לֶקַח טוֹב נָתַתִּי לָכֶם תּוֹרָתִי אַל־תַּעֲזֹבוּ׃

3 Once I was a son to my father, The tender darling of my mother.

ג כִּי־בֵן הָיִיתִי לְאָבִי רַךְ וְיָחִיד לִפְנֵי אִמִּי׃

kee VAYN ha-YEE-tee l'-a-VEE RAKH v'-ya-KHEED lif-NAY i-MEE

4 He instructed me and said to me, "Let your mind hold on to my words; Keep my commandments and you will live.

ד וַיֹּרֵנִי וַיֹּאמֶר לִי יִתְמָךְ־דְּבָרַי לִבֶּךָ שְׁמֹר מִצְוֹתַי וֶחְיֵה׃

5 Acquire wisdom, acquire discernment; Do not forget and do not swerve from my words.

ה קְנֵה חָכְמָה קְנֵה בִינָה אַל־תִּשְׁכַּח וְאַל־תֵּט מֵאִמְרֵי־פִי׃

6 Do not forsake her and she will guard you; Love her and she will protect you.

ו אַל־תַּעַזְבֶהָ וְתִשְׁמְרֶךָּ אֱהָבֶהָ וְתִצְּרֶךָּ׃

7 The beginning of wisdom is – acquire wisdom; With all your acquisitions, acquire discernment.

ז רֵאשִׁית חָכְמָה קְנֵה חָכְמָה וּבְכָל־קִנְיָנְךָ קְנֵה בִינָה׃

8 Hug her to you and she will exalt you; She will bring you honor if you embrace her.

ח סַלְסְלֶהָ וּתְרוֹמְמֶךָּ תְּכַבֵּדְךָ כִּי תְחַבְּקֶנָּה׃

9 She will adorn your head with a graceful wreath; Crown you with a glorious diadem."

ט תִּתֵּן לְרֹאשְׁךָ לִוְיַת־חֵן עֲטֶרֶת תִּפְאֶרֶת תְּמַגְּנֶךָּ׃

10 My son, heed and take in my words, And you will have many years of life.

י שְׁמַע בְּנִי וְקַח אֲמָרָי וְיִרְבּוּ לְךָ שְׁנוֹת חַיִּים׃

A father teaching his son the prayers at the Western Wall

4:3 Once I was a son to my father Although this verse can be understood literally, it also contains a parable. The speaker represents the Nation of Israel, described in the Bible (Exodus 4:22) as *Hashem*'s firstborn son. It is to that chosen child that God imparts the wisdom of His *Torah*, just as a father imparts precious wisdom to his son (see verse 4). Like the child in this verse, the Nation of Israel received the *Torah* at a tender stage, shortly after being released from the bondage of Egypt.

6

11 I instruct you in the way of wisdom; I guide you in straight courses.	בְּדֶרֶךְ חָכְמָה הֹרֵתִיךָ הִדְרַכְתִּיךָ בְּמַעְגְּלֵי־יֹשֶׁר׃ יא

11 I instruct you in the way of wisdom; I guide you in straight courses.

בְּדֶרֶךְ חָכְמָה הֹרֵתִיךָ הִדְרַכְתִּיךָ בְּמַעְגְּלֵי־יֹשֶׁר׃ יא

12 You will walk without breaking stride; When you run, you will not stumble.

בְּלֶכְתְּךָ לֹא־יֵצַר צַעֲדֶךָ וְאִם־תָּרוּץ לֹא תִכָּשֵׁל׃ יב

13 Hold fast to discipline; do not let go; Keep it; it is your life.

הַחֲזֵק בַּמּוּסָר אַל־תֶּרֶף נִצְּרֶהָ כִּי־הִיא חַיֶּיךָ׃ יג

14 Do not enter on the path of the wicked; Do not walk on the way of evil men.

בְּאֹרַח רְשָׁעִים אַל־תָּבֹא וְאַל־תְּאַשֵּׁר בְּדֶרֶךְ רָעִים׃ יד

15 Avoid it; do not pass through it; Turn away from it; pass it by.

פְּרָעֵהוּ אַל־תַּעֲבָר־בּוֹ שְׂטֵה מֵעָלָיו וַעֲבוֹר׃ טו

16 For they cannot sleep unless they have done evil; Unless they make someone fall they are robbed of sleep.

כִּי לֹא יִשְׁנוּ אִם־לֹא יָרֵעוּ וְנִגְזְלָה שְׁנָתָם אִם־לֹא יכשולו [יַכְשִׁילוּ]׃ טז

17 They eat the bread of wickedness And drink the wine of lawlessness.

כִּי לָחֲמוּ לֶחֶם רֶשַׁע וְיֵין חֲמָסִים יִשְׁתּוּ׃ יז

18 The path of the righteous is like radiant sunlight, Ever brightening until noon.

וְאֹרַח צַדִּיקִים כְּאוֹר נֹגַהּ הוֹלֵךְ וָאוֹר עַד־נְכוֹן הַיּוֹם׃ יח

19 The way of the wicked is all darkness; They do not know what will make them stumble.

דֶּרֶךְ רְשָׁעִים כַּאֲפֵלָה לֹא יָדְעוּ בַּמֶּה יִכָּשֵׁלוּ׃ יט

20 My son, listen to my speech; Incline your ear to my words.

בְּנִי לִדְבָרַי הַקְשִׁיבָה לַאֲמָרַי הַט־אָזְנֶךָ׃ כ

21 Do not lose sight of them; Keep them in your mind.

אַל־יַלִּיזוּ מֵעֵינֶיךָ שָׁמְרֵם בְּתוֹךְ לְבָבֶךָ׃ כא

22 They are life to him who finds them, Healing for his whole body.

כִּי־חַיִּים הֵם לְמֹצְאֵיהֶם וּלְכָל־בְּשָׂרוֹ מַרְפֵּא׃ כב

23 More than all that you guard, guard your mind, For it is the source of life.

מִכָּל־מִשְׁמָר נְצֹר לִבֶּךָ כִּי־מִמֶּנּוּ תּוֹצְאוֹת חַיִּים׃ כג

24 Put crooked speech away from you; Keep devious talk far from you.

הָסֵר מִמְּךָ עִקְּשׁוּת פֶּה וּלְזוּת שְׂפָתַיִם הַרְחֵק מִמֶּךָּ׃ כד

25 Let your eyes look forward, Your gaze be straight ahead.

עֵינֶיךָ לְנֹכַח יַבִּיטוּ וְעַפְעַפֶּיךָ יַיְשִׁרוּ נֶגְדֶּךָ׃ כה

26 Survey the course you take, And all your ways will prosper.

פַּלֵּס מַעְגַּל רַגְלֶךָ וְכָל־דְּרָכֶיךָ יִכֹּנוּ׃ כו

27 Do not swerve to the right or the left; Keep your feet from evil.

אַל־תֵּט־יָמִין וּשְׂמֹאול הָסֵר רַגְלְךָ מֵרָע׃ כז

5 ¹ My son, listen to my wisdom; Incline your ear to my insight,

בְּנִי לְחָכְמָתִי הַקְשִׁיבָה לִתְבוּנָתִי הַט־אָזְנֶךָ׃ א ה

² That you may have foresight, While your lips hold fast to knowledge.

לִשְׁמֹר מְזִמּוֹת וְדַעַת שְׂפָתֶיךָ יִנְצֹרוּ׃ ב

³ For the lips of a forbidden woman drip honey; Her mouth is smoother than oil;

גּ כִּי נֹפֶת תִּטֹּפְנָה שִׂפְתֵי זָרָה וְחָלָק מִשֶּׁמֶן חִכָּהּ:

⁴ But in the end she is as bitter as wormwood, Sharp as a two-edged sword.

ד וְאַחֲרִיתָהּ מָרָה כַלַּעֲנָה חַדָּה כְּחֶרֶב פִּיּוֹת:

⁵ Her feet go down to Death; Her steps take hold of Sheol.

ה רַגְלֶיהָ יֹרְדוֹת מָוֶת שְׁאוֹל צְעָדֶיהָ יִתְמֹכוּ:

⁶ She does not chart a path of life; Her course meanders for lack of knowledge.

ו אֹרַח חַיִּים פֶּן־תְּפַלֵּס נָעוּ מַעְגְּלֹתֶיהָ לֹא תֵדָע:

⁷ So now, sons, pay heed to me, And do not swerve from the words of my mouth.

ז וְעַתָּה בָנִים שִׁמְעוּ־לִי וְאַל־תָּסוּרוּ מֵאִמְרֵי־פִי:

⁸ Keep yourself far away from her; Do not come near the doorway of her house

ח הַרְחֵק מֵעָלֶיהָ דַרְכֶּךָ וְאַל־תִּקְרַב אֶל־פֶּתַח בֵּיתָהּ:

⁹ Lest you give up your vigor to others, Your years to a ruthless one;

ט פֶּן־תִּתֵּן לַאֲחֵרִים הוֹדֶךָ וּשְׁנֹתֶיךָ לְאַכְזָרִי:

¹⁰ Lest strangers eat their fill of your strength, And your toil be for the house of another;

י פֶּן־יִשְׂבְּעוּ זָרִים כֹּחֶךָ וַעֲצָבֶיךָ בְּבֵית נָכְרִי:

¹¹ And in the end you roar, When your flesh and body are consumed,

יא וְנָהַמְתָּ בְאַחֲרִיתֶךָ בִּכְלוֹת בְּשָׂרְךָ וּשְׁאֵרֶךָ:

¹² And say, "O how I hated discipline, And heartily spurned rebuke.

יב וְאָמַרְתָּ אֵיךְ שָׂנֵאתִי מוּסָר וְתוֹכַחַת נָאַץ לִבִּי:

¹³ I did not pay heed to my teachers, Or incline my ear to my instructors.

יג וְלֹא־שָׁמַעְתִּי בְּקוֹל מוֹרָי וְלִמְלַמְּדַי לֹא־הִטִּיתִי אָזְנִי:

¹⁴ Soon I was in dire trouble Amidst the assembled congregation."

יד כִּמְעַט הָיִיתִי בְכָל־רָע בְּתוֹךְ קָהָל וְעֵדָה:

¹⁵ Drink water from your own cistern, Running water from your own well.

טו שְׁתֵה־מַיִם מִבּוֹרֶךָ וְנֹזְלִים מִתּוֹךְ בְּאֵרֶךָ:

¹⁶ Your springs will gush forth In streams in the public squares.

טז יָפוּצוּ מַעְיְנֹתֶיךָ חוּצָה בָּרְחֹבוֹת פַּלְגֵי־מָיִם:

¹⁷ They will be yours alone, Others having no part with you.

יז יִהְיוּ־לְךָ לְבַדֶּךָ וְאֵין לְזָרִים אִתָּךְ:

¹⁸ Let your fountain be blessed; Find joy in the wife of your youth –

יח יְהִי־מְקוֹרְךָ בָרוּךְ וּשְׂמַח מֵאֵשֶׁת נְעוּרֶךָ:

y'-HEE m'-ko-r'-KHA va-RUKH us-MAKH may-AY-shet n'-u-RE-kha

Proverbs

5:18 Find joy in the wife of your youth King *Shlomo* compares the wife of one's youth to a fountain, a source of life-giving water, because she is a source of continued life through the children she bears. Water is a precious commodity in Israel, as rain falls in unpredictable and sometimes limited quantities, and only in its season. Being dependent on the Lord for rain ensures that His children must maintain a close connection with Him in the Land of Israel, and recognize the He is the true source of life and all of its blessings.

The *Tel Aviv* promenade after the rain

19 A loving doe, a graceful mountain goat. Let her breasts satisfy you at all times; Be infatuated with love of her always.

יט אַיֶּלֶת אֲהָבִים וְיַעֲלַת־חֵן דַּדֶּיהָ יְרַוֻּךָ בְכָל־עֵת בְּאַהֲבָתָהּ תִּשְׁגֶּה תָמִיד:

20 Why be infatuated, my son, with a forbidden woman? Why clasp the bosom of an alien woman?

כ וְלָמָּה תִשְׁגֶּה בְנִי בְזָרָה וּתְחַבֵּק חֵק נָכְרִיָּה:

21 For a man's ways are before the eyes of *Hashem*; He surveys his entire course.

כא כִּי נֹכַח עֵינֵי יְהוָה דַּרְכֵי־אִישׁ וְכָל־מַעְגְּלֹתָיו מְפַלֵּס:

22 The wicked man will be trapped in his iniquities; He will be caught up in the ropes of his sin.

כב עֲווֹנוֹתָיו יִלְכְּדֻנוֹ אֶת־הָרָשָׁע וּבְחַבְלֵי חַטָּאתוֹ יִתָּמֵךְ:

23 He will die for lack of discipline, Infatuated by his great folly.

כג הוּא יָמוּת בְּאֵין מוּסָר וּבְרֹב אִוַּלְתּוֹ יִשְׁגֶּה:

6 1 My son, if you have stood surety for your fellow, Given your hand for another,

א בְּנִי אִם־עָרַבְתָּ לְרֵעֶךָ תָּקַעְתָּ לַזָּר כַּפֶּיךָ:

2 You have been trapped by the words of your mouth, Snared by the words of your mouth.

ב נוֹקַשְׁתָּ בְאִמְרֵי־פִיךָ נִלְכַּדְתָּ בְּאִמְרֵי־פִיךָ:

3 Do this, then, my son, to extricate yourself, For you have come into the power of your fellow: Go grovel – and badger your fellow;

ג עֲשֵׂה זֹאת אֵפוֹא בְּנִי וְהִנָּצֵל כִּי בָאתָ בְכַף־רֵעֶךָ לֵךְ הִתְרַפֵּס וּרְהַב רֵעֶיךָ:

4 Give your eyes no sleep, Your pupils no slumber.

ד אַל־תִּתֵּן שֵׁנָה לְעֵינֶיךָ וּתְנוּמָה לְעַפְעַפֶּיךָ:

5 Save yourself like a deer out of the hand [of a hunter], Like a bird out of the hand of a fowler.

ה הִנָּצֵל כִּצְבִי מִיָּד וּכְצִפּוֹר מִיַּד יָקוּשׁ:

6 Lazybones, go to the ant; Study its ways and learn.

ו לֵךְ־אֶל־נְמָלָה עָצֵל רְאֵה דְרָכֶיהָ וַחֲכָם:

7 Without leaders, officers, or rulers,

ז אֲשֶׁר אֵין־לָהּ קָצִין שֹׁטֵר וּמֹשֵׁל:

8 It lays up its stores during the summer, Gathers in its food at the harvest.

ח תָּכִין בַּקַּיִץ לַחְמָהּ אָגְרָה בַקָּצִיר מַאֲכָלָהּ:

9 How long will you lie there, lazybones; When will you wake from your sleep?

ט עַד־מָתַי עָצֵל תִּשְׁכָּב מָתַי תָּקוּם מִשְּׁנָתֶךָ:

10 A bit more sleep, a bit more slumber, A bit more hugging yourself in bed,

י מְעַט שֵׁנוֹת מְעַט תְּנוּמוֹת מְעַט חִבֻּק יָדַיִם לִשְׁכָּב:

11 And poverty will come calling upon you, And want, like a man with a shield.

יא וּבָא־כִמְהַלֵּךְ רֵאשֶׁךָ וּמַחְסֹרְךָ כְּאִישׁ מָגֵן:

12 A scoundrel, an evil man Lives by crooked speech,

יב אָדָם בְּלִיַּעַל אִישׁ אָוֶן הוֹלֵךְ עִקְּשׁוּת פֶּה:

13 Winking his eyes, Shuffling his feet, Pointing his finger.

יג קֹרֵץ בְּעֵינָו מֹלֵל בְּרַגְלָו מֹרֶה בְּאֶצְבְּעֹתָיו:

14 Duplicity is in his heart; He plots evil all the time; He incites quarrels.

יד תַּהְפֻּכוֹת בְּלִבּוֹ חֹרֵשׁ רָע בְּכָל־עֵת מדנים [מִדְיָנִים] יְשַׁלֵּחַ:

Proverbs

9

¹⁵ Therefore calamity will come upon him without warning; Suddenly he will be broken beyond repair.

עַל־כֵּן פִּתְאֹם יָבוֹא אֵידוֹ פֶּתַע יִשָּׁבֵר וְאֵין מַרְפֵּא: טו

¹⁶ Six things *Hashem* hates; Seven are an abomination to Him:

שֶׁשׁ־הֵנָּה שָׂנֵא יְהוָה וְשֶׁבַע תּוֹעֲבוֹת [תּוֹעֲבַת] נַפְשׁוֹ: טז

¹⁷ A haughty bearing, A lying tongue, Hands that shed innocent blood,

עֵינַיִם רָמוֹת לְשׁוֹן שָׁקֶר וְיָדַיִם שֹׁפְכוֹת דָּם־נָקִי: יז

¹⁸ A mind that hatches evil plots, Feet quick to run to evil,

לֵב חֹרֵשׁ מַחְשְׁבוֹת אָוֶן רַגְלַיִם מְמַהֲרוֹת לָרוּץ לָרָעָה: יח

¹⁹ A false witness testifying lies, And one who incites brothers to quarrel.

יָפִיחַ כְּזָבִים עֵד שָׁקֶר וּמְשַׁלֵּחַ מְדָנִים בֵּין אַחִים: יט

²⁰ My son, keep your father's commandment; Do not forsake your mother's teaching.

נְצֹר בְּנִי מִצְוַת אָבִיךָ וְאַל־תִּטֹּשׁ תּוֹרַת אִמֶּךָ: כ

²¹ Tie them over your heart always; Bind them around your throat.

קָשְׁרֵם עַל־לִבְּךָ תָמִיד עָנְדֵם עַל־גַּרְגְּרֹתֶךָ: כא

²² When you walk it will lead you; When you lie down it will watch over you; And when you are awake it will talk with you.

בְּהִתְהַלֶּכְךָ תַּנְחֶה אֹתָךְ בְּשָׁכְבְּךָ תִּשְׁמֹר עָלֶיךָ וַהֲקִיצוֹתָ הִיא תְשִׂיחֶךָ: כב

²³ For the commandment is a lamp, The teaching is a light, And the way to life is the rebuke that disciplines.

כִּי נֵר מִצְוָה וְתוֹרָה אוֹר וְדֶרֶךְ חַיִּים תּוֹכְחוֹת מוּסָר: כג

KEE NAYR mitz-VAH v'-TO-rah OR v'-DE-rekh kha-YEEM to-kh'-KHOT mu-SAR

²⁴ It will keep you from an evil woman, From the smooth tongue of a forbidden woman.

לִשְׁמָרְךָ מֵאֵשֶׁת רָע מֵחֶלְקַת לָשׁוֹן נָכְרִיָּה: כד

²⁵ Do not lust for her beauty Or let her captivate you with her eyes.

אַל־תַּחְמֹד יָפְיָהּ בִּלְבָבֶךָ וְאַל־תִּקָּחֲךָ בְּעַפְעַפֶּיהָ: כה

²⁶ The last loaf of bread will go for a harlot; A married woman will snare a person of honor.

כִּי בְעַד־אִשָּׁה זוֹנָה עַד־כִּכַּר לָחֶם וְאֵשֶׁת אִישׁ נֶפֶשׁ יְקָרָה תָצוּד: כו

²⁷ Can a man rake embers into his bosom Without burning his clothes?

הֲיַחְתֶּה אִישׁ אֵשׁ בְּחֵיקוֹ וּבְגָדָיו לֹא תִשָּׂרַפְנָה: כז

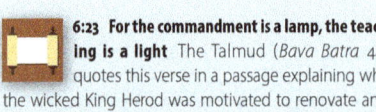 **6:23 For the commandment is a lamp, the teaching is a light** The Talmud (*Bava Batra* 4a) quotes this verse in a passage explaining why the wicked King Herod was motivated to renovate and beautify the second *Beit Hamikdash*. Herod had engaged in a murderous rampage against the leading rabbis of his generation, only to regret his evil actions after he came to know and respect the Sage *Bava ben Buta*. "What can I do to repent my evil ways?" King Herod begged *Bava*. Quoting this verse, *Bava* responded, "You who extinguished the light of the world by killing so many Torah scholars, can atone by bringing more light into the world." Herod listened to the rabbi and immediately embarked upon a massive architectural project, restoring the glory of the *Beit Hamikdash*, and causing the second Temple to surpass even the beauty of the first Temple built by King *Shlomo*. In this way, he strengthened the light emanating to the world.

Model of Herod's Temple, *Yerushalayim*

28 Can a man walk on live coals Without scorching his feet?

כח אִם־יְהַלֵּךְ אִישׁ עַל־הַגֶּחָלִים וְרַגְלָיו לֹא תִכָּוֶינָה:

29 It is the same with one who sleeps with his fellow's wife; None who touches her will go unpunished.

כט כֵּן הַבָּא אֶל־אֵשֶׁת רֵעֵהוּ לֹא יִנָּקֶה כָּל־הַנֹּגֵעַ בָּהּ:

30 A thief is not held in contempt For stealing to appease his hunger;

ל לֹא־יָבוּזוּ לַגַּנָּב כִּי יִגְנוֹב לְמַלֵּא נַפְשׁוֹ כִּי יִרְעָב:

31 Yet if caught he must pay sevenfold; He must give up all he owns.

לא וְנִמְצָא יְשַׁלֵּם שִׁבְעָתָיִם אֶת־כָּל־הוֹן בֵּיתוֹ יִתֵּן:

32 He who commits adultery is devoid of sense; Only one who would destroy himself does such a thing.

לב נֹאֵף אִשָּׁה חֲסַר־לֵב מַשְׁחִית נַפְשׁוֹ הוּא יַעֲשֶׂנָּה:

33 He will meet with disease and disgrace; His reproach will never be expunged.

לג נֶגַע־וְקָלוֹן יִמְצָא וְחֶרְפָּתוֹ לֹא תִמָּחֶה:

34 The fury of the husband will be passionate; He will show no pity on his day of vengeance.

לד כִּי־קִנְאָה חֲמַת־גָּבֶר וְלֹא־יַחְמוֹל בְּיוֹם נָקָם:

35 He will not have regard for any ransom; He will refuse your bribe, however great.

לה לֹא־יִשָּׂא פְּנֵי כָל־כֹּפֶר וְלֹא־יֹאבֶה כִּי תַרְבֶּה־שֹׁחַד:

7 1 My son, heed my words; And store up my commandments with you.

ז א בְּנִי שְׁמֹר אֲמָרָי וּמִצְוֹתַי תִּצְפֹּן אִתָּךְ:

2 Keep my commandments and live, My teaching, as the apple of your eye.

ב שְׁמֹר מִצְוֹתַי וֶחְיֵה וְתוֹרָתִי כְּאִישׁוֹן עֵינֶיךָ:

3 Bind them on your fingers; Write them on the tablet of your mind.

ג קָשְׁרֵם עַל־אֶצְבְּעֹתֶיךָ כָּתְבֵם עַל־לוּחַ לִבֶּךָ:

4 Say to Wisdom, "You are my sister," And call Understanding a kinswoman.

ד אֱמֹר לַחָכְמָה אֲחֹתִי אָתְּ וּמֹדָע לַבִּינָה תִקְרָא:

5 She will guard you from a forbidden woman; From an alien woman whose talk is smooth.

ה לִשְׁמָרְךָ מֵאִשָּׁה זָרָה מִנָּכְרִיָּה אֲמָרֶיהָ הֶחֱלִיקָה:

6 From the window of my house, Through my lattice, I looked out

ו כִּי בְּחַלּוֹן בֵּיתִי בְּעַד אֶשְׁנַבִּי נִשְׁקָפְתִּי:

7 And saw among the simple, Noticed among the youths, A lad devoid of sense.

ז וָאֵרֶא בַפְּתָאיִם אָבִינָה בַבָּנִים נַעַר חֲסַר־לֵב:

8 He was crossing the street near her corner, Walking toward her house

ח עֹבֵר בַּשּׁוּק אֵצֶל פִּנָּהּ וְדֶרֶךְ בֵּיתָהּ יִצְעָד:

9 In the dusk of evening, In the dark hours of night.

ט בְּנֶשֶׁף־בְּעֶרֶב יוֹם בְּאִישׁוֹן לַיְלָה וַאֲפֵלָה:

10 A woman comes toward him Dressed like a harlot, with set purpose.

י וְהִנֵּה אִשָּׁה לִקְרָאתוֹ שִׁית זוֹנָה וּנְצֻרַת לֵב:

11 She is bustling and restive; She is never at home.

יא הֹמִיָּה הִיא וְסֹרָרֶת בְּבֵיתָהּ לֹא־יִשְׁכְּנוּ רַגְלֶיהָ:

12 Now in the street, now in the square, She lurks at every corner.

יב פַּעַם בַּחוּץ פַּעַם בָּרְחֹבוֹת וְאֵצֶל כָּל־פִּנָּה תֶאֱרֹב:

13 She lays hold of him and kisses him; Brazenly she says to him,

וְהֶחֱזִיקָה בּוֹ וְנָשְׁקָה־לוֹ הֵעֵזָה פָנֶיהָ וַתֹּאמַר לוֹ: יג

14 "I had to make a sacrifice of well-being; Today I fulfilled my vows.

זִבְחֵי שְׁלָמִים עָלָי הַיּוֹם שִׁלַּמְתִּי נְדָרָי: יד

ziv-KHAY sh'-la-MEEM a-LAI ha-YOM shi-LAM-tee n'-da-RAI

15 Therefore I have come out to you, Seeking you, and have found you.

עַל־כֵּן יָצָאתִי לִקְרָאתֶךָ לְשַׁחֵר פָּנֶיךָ וָאֶמְצָאֶךָּ: טו

16 I have decked my couch with covers Of dyed Egyptian linen;

מַרְבַדִּים רָבַדְתִּי עַרְשִׂי חֲטֻבוֹת אֵטוּן מִצְרָיִם: טז

17 I have sprinkled my bed With myrrh, aloes, and cinnamon.

נַפְתִּי מִשְׁכָּבִי מֹר אֲהָלִים וְקִנָּמוֹן: יז

18 Let us drink our fill of love till morning; Let us delight in amorous embrace.

לְכָה נִרְוֶה דֹדִים עַד־הַבֹּקֶר נִתְעַלְּסָה בָּאֳהָבִים: יח

19 For the man of the house is away; He is off on a distant journey.

כִּי אֵין הָאִישׁ בְּבֵיתוֹ הָלַךְ בְּדֶרֶךְ מֵרָחוֹק: יט

20 He took his bag of money with him And will return only at mid-month."

צְרוֹר־הַכֶּסֶף לָקַח בְּיָדוֹ לְיוֹם הַכֵּסֶא יָבֹא בֵיתוֹ: כ

21 She sways him with her eloquence, Turns him aside with her smooth talk.

הִטַּתּוּ בְּרֹב לִקְחָהּ בְּחֵלֶק שְׂפָתֶיהָ תַּדִּיחֶנּוּ: כא

22 Thoughtlessly he follows her, Like an ox going to the slaughter, Like a fool to the stocks for punishment –

הוֹלֵךְ אַחֲרֶיהָ פִּתְאֹם כְּשׁוֹר אֶל־טֶבַח יָבֹא וּכְעֶכֶס אֶל־מוּסַר אֱוִיל: כב

23 Until the arrow pierces his liver. He is like a bird rushing into a trap, Not knowing his life is at stake.

עַד יְפַלַּח חֵץ כְּבֵדוֹ כְּמַהֵר צִפּוֹר אֶל־פָּח וְלֹא־יָדַע כִּי־בְנַפְשׁוֹ הוּא: כג

24 Now, sons, listen to me; Pay attention to my words;

וְעַתָּה בָנִים שִׁמְעוּ־לִי וְהַקְשִׁיבוּ לְאִמְרֵי־פִי: כד

25 Let your mind not wander down her ways; Do not stray onto her paths.

אַל־יֵשְׂטְ אֶל־דְּרָכֶיהָ לִבֶּךָ אַל־תֵּתַע בִּנְתִיבוֹתֶיהָ: כה

26 For many are those she has struck dead, And numerous are her victims.

כִּי־רַבִּים חֲלָלִים הִפִּילָה וַעֲצֻמִים כָּל־הֲרֻגֶיהָ: כו

 7:14 Sacrifice of well-being The sacrifice of well-being is often called the 'peace-offering' based on its Hebrew name, *korban sh'lamim* (קרבן שלמים), which is related to the Hebrew word *shalom* (שלום), 'peace.' According to Jewish tradition, it is called this because the *korban sh'lamim* symbolizes peace and unity, as it is the only offering that is shared by all relevant parties: *Hashem*, via the portions burned on the altar, and the priest and the owner of the

Yerushalayim

sacrifice who each consume part of the meat. It is not a coincidence that this is also the only offering that is not restricted to the *Beit Hamikdash*, but may be eaten anywhere in the city of Jerusalem. The Hebrew name for Jerusalem, *Yerushalayim*, also has the word *shalom* at its root, and indeed, Jerusalem is known as *ir shel shalom*, the city of peace. *Yerushalayim* is meant to be the source for all peace on earth, and is therefore closely connected with the well-being offering.

קרבן שלמים

27 Her house is a highway to Sheol Leading down to Death's inner chambers.

כז דְּרָכֵי שְׁאוֹל בֵּיתָהּ יֹרְדוֹת אֶל־חַדְרֵי־מָוֶת:

8 ¹ It is Wisdom calling, Understanding raising her voice.

ח א הֲלֹא־חָכְמָה תִקְרָא וּתְבוּנָה תִּתֵּן קוֹלָהּ:

² She takes her stand at the topmost heights, By the wayside, at the crossroads,

ב בְּרֹאשׁ־מְרוֹמִים עֲלֵי־דָרֶךְ בֵּית נְתִיבוֹת נִצָּבָה:

³ Near the gates at the city entrance; At the entryways, she shouts,

ג לְיַד־שְׁעָרִים לְפִי־קָרֶת מְבוֹא פְתָחִים תָּרֹנָּה:

⁴ "O men, I call to you; My cry is to all mankind.

ד אֲלֵיכֶם אִישִׁים אֶקְרָא וְקוֹלִי אֶל־בְּנֵי אָדָם:

⁵ O simple ones, learn shrewdness; O dullards, instruct your minds.

ה הָבִינוּ פְתָאיִם עָרְמָה וּכְסִילִים הָבִינוּ לֵב:

⁶ Listen, for I speak noble things; Uprightness comes from my lips;

ו שִׁמְעוּ כִּי־נְגִידִים אֲדַבֵּר וּמִפְתַּח שְׂפָתַי מֵישָׁרִים:

⁷ My mouth utters truth; Wickedness is abhorrent to my lips.

ז כִּי־אֱמֶת יֶהְגֶּה חִכִּי וְתוֹעֲבַת שְׂפָתַי רֶשַׁע:

⁸ All my words are just, None of them perverse or crooked;

ח בְּצֶדֶק כָּל־אִמְרֵי־פִי אֵין בָּהֶם נִפְתָּל וְעִקֵּשׁ:

⁹ All are straightforward to the intelligent man, And right to those who have attained knowledge.

ט כֻּלָּם נְכֹחִים לַמֵּבִין וִישָׁרִים לְמֹצְאֵי דָעַת:

¹⁰ Accept my discipline rather than silver, Knowledge rather than choice gold.

י קְחוּ־מוּסָרִי וְאַל־כָּסֶף וְדַעַת מֵחָרוּץ נִבְחָר:

¹¹ For wisdom is better than rubies; No goods can equal her.

יא כִּי־טוֹבָה חָכְמָה מִפְּנִינִים וְכָל־חֲפָצִים לֹא יִשְׁווּ־בָהּ:

¹² "I, Wisdom, live with Prudence; I attain knowledge and foresight.

יב אֲנִי־חָכְמָה שָׁכַנְתִּי עָרְמָה וְדַעַת מְזִמּוֹת אֶמְצָא:

¹³ To fear *Hashem* is to hate evil; I hate pride, arrogance, the evil way, And duplicity in speech.

יג יִרְאַת יְהֹוָה שְׂנֹאת רָע גֵּאָה וְגָאוֹן וְדֶרֶךְ רָע וּפִי תַהְפֻּכוֹת שָׂנֵאתִי:

¹⁴ Mine are counsel and resourcefulness; I am understanding; courage is mine.

יד לִי־עֵצָה וְתוּשִׁיָּה אֲנִי בִינָה לִי גְבוּרָה:

¹⁵ Through me kings reign And rulers decree just laws;

טו בִּי מְלָכִים יִמְלֹכוּ וְרוֹזְנִים יְחֹקְקוּ צֶדֶק:

¹⁶ Through me princes rule, Great men and all the righteous judges.

טז בִּי שָׂרִים יָשֹׂרוּ וּנְדִיבִים כָּל־שֹׁפְטֵי צֶדֶק:

¹⁷ Those who love me I love, And those who seek me will find me.

יז אֲנִי אֹהֲבֶיהָ [אֹהֲבַי] אֵהָב וּמְשַׁחֲרַי יִמְצָאֻנְנִי:

¹⁸ Riches and honor belong to me, Enduring wealth and success.

יח עֹשֶׁר־וְכָבוֹד אִתִּי הוֹן עָתֵק וּצְדָקָה:

19 My fruit is better than gold, fine gold, And my produce better than choice silver.

יט טוֹב פִּרְיִי מֵחָרוּץ וּמִפָּז וּתְבוּאָתִי מִכֶּסֶף נִבְחָר:

20 I walk on the way of righteousness, On the paths of justice.

כ בְּאֹרַח־צְדָקָה אֲהַלֵּךְ בְּתוֹךְ נְתִיבוֹת מִשְׁפָּט:

21 I endow those who love me with substance; I will fill their treasuries.

כא לְהַנְחִיל אֹהֲבַי יֵשׁ וְאֹצְרֹתֵיהֶם אֲמַלֵּא:

22 *"Hashem* created me at the beginning of His course As the first of His works of old.

כב יְהוָה קָנָנִי רֵאשִׁית דַּרְכּוֹ קֶדֶם מִפְעָלָיו מֵאָז:

a-do-NAI ka-NA-nee ray-SHEET dar-KO KE-dem mif-a-LAV may-AZ

23 In the distant past I was fashioned, At the beginning, at the origin of earth.

כג מֵעוֹלָם נִסַּכְתִּי מֵרֹאשׁ מִקַּדְמֵי־אָרֶץ:

24 There was still no deep when I was brought forth, No springs rich in water;

כד בְּאֵין־תְּהֹמוֹת חוֹלָלְתִּי בְּאֵין מַעְיָנוֹת נִכְבַּדֵּי־מָיִם:

25 Before [the foundation of] the mountains were sunk, Before the hills I was born.

כה בְּטֶרֶם הָרִים הָטְבָּעוּ לִפְנֵי גְבָעוֹת חוֹלָלְתִּי:

26 He had not yet made earth and fields, Or the world's first clumps of clay.

כו עַד־לֹא עָשָׂה אֶרֶץ וְחוּצוֹת וְרֹאשׁ עַפְרוֹת תֵּבֵל:

27 I was there when He set the heavens into place; When He fixed the horizon upon the deep;

כז בַּהֲכִינוֹ שָׁמַיִם שָׁם אָנִי בְּחֻקוֹ חוּג עַל־פְּנֵי תְהוֹם:

28 When He made the heavens above firm, And the fountains of the deep gushed forth;

כח בְּאַמְּצוֹ שְׁחָקִים מִמָּעַל בַּעֲזוֹז עִינוֹת תְּהוֹם:

29 When He assigned the sea its limits, So that its waters never transgress His command; When He fixed the foundations of the earth,

כט בְּשׂוּמוֹ לַיָּם חֻקּוֹ וּמַיִם לֹא יַעַבְרוּ־פִּיו בְּחוּקוֹ מוֹסְדֵי אָרֶץ:

30 I was with Him as a confidant, A source of delight every day, Rejoicing before Him at all times,

ל וָאֶהְיֶה אֶצְלוֹ אָמוֹן וָאֶהְיֶה שַׁעֲשֻׁעִים יוֹם יוֹם מְשַׂחֶקֶת לְפָנָיו בְּכָל־עֵת:

31 Rejoicing in His inhabited world, Finding delight with mankind.

לא מְשַׂחֶקֶת בְּתֵבֵל אַרְצוֹ וְשַׁעֲשֻׁעַי אֶת־בְּנֵי אָדָם:

32 Now, sons, listen to me; Happy are they who keep my ways.

לב וְעַתָּה בָנִים שִׁמְעוּ־לִי וְאַשְׁרֵי דְּרָכַי יִשְׁמֹרוּ:

33 Heed discipline and become wise; Do not spurn it.

לג שִׁמְעוּ מוּסָר וַחֲכָמוּ וְאַל־תִּפְרָעוּ:

34 Happy is the man who listens to me, Coming early to my gates each day, Waiting outside my doors.

לד אַשְׁרֵי אָדָם שֹׁמֵעַ לִי לִשְׁקֹד עַל־דַּלְתֹתַי יוֹם יוֹם לִשְׁמֹר מְזוּזֹת פְּתָחָי:

Reading from the *Torah* at the Western Wall

8:22 The beginning of His course The wisdom of the *Torah* is described in this verse as the "beginning of His course." The Hebrew word for 'beginning,' re-ishit (ראשית), is also used to describe the Children of Israel, called *reisheet t'vuato*, 'the first-fruits of His [*Hashem's*] harvest' (Jeremiah 2:3), and it is also the first word of *Sefer Bereishit*, describing the creation of the world. The Sages connect the three uses of this word and teach that *Hashem* created the world for the sake of Israel and of the *Torah*. God created a world in which the Children of Israel are to follow the *Torah*, and thereby serve as a model for the rest of the nations.

ראשית

Proverbs

Proverbs

35 For he who finds me finds life And obtains favor from *Hashem*.

לה כִּי מֹצְאִי מָצָא [מָצָא] חַיִּים וַיָּפֶק רָצוֹן מֵיְהֹוָה:

36 But he who misses me destroys himself; All who hate me love death."

לו וְחֹטְאִי חֹמֵס נַפְשׁוֹ כָּל־מְשַׂנְאַי אָהֲבוּ מָוֶת:

9 ¹ Wisdom has built her house, She has hewn her seven pillars.

ט א חָכְמוֹת בָּנְתָה בֵיתָהּ חָצְבָה עַמּוּדֶיהָ שִׁבְעָה:

khokh-MOT ba-n'-TAH vay-TAH kha-tz'-VAH a-mu-DE-ha shiv-AH

² She has prepared the feast, Mixed the wine, And also set the table.

ב טָבְחָה טִבְחָהּ מָסְכָה יֵינָהּ אַף עָרְכָה שֻׁלְחָנָהּ:

³ She has sent out her maids to announce On the heights of the town,

ג שָׁלְחָה נַעֲרֹתֶיהָ תִקְרָא עַל־גַּפֵּי מְרֹמֵי קָרֶת:

⁴ "Let the simple enter here"; To those devoid of sense she says,

ד מִי־פֶתִי יָסֻר הֵנָּה חֲסַר־לֵב אָמְרָה לּוֹ:

⁵ "Come, eat my food And drink the wine that I have mixed;

ה לְכוּ לַחֲמוּ בְלַחֲמִי וּשְׁתוּ בְּיַיִן מָסָכְתִּי:

⁶ Give up simpleness and live, Walk in the way of understanding."

ו עִזְבוּ פְתָאיִם וִחְיוּ וְאִשְׁרוּ בְּדֶרֶךְ בִּינָה:

⁷ To correct a scoffer, Or rebuke a wicked man for his blemish, Is to call down abuse on oneself.*

ז יֹסֵר לֵץ לֹקֵחַ לוֹ קָלוֹן וּמוֹכִיחַ לְרָשָׁע מוּמוֹ:

⁸ Do not rebuke a scoffer, for he will hate you; Reprove a wise man, and he will love you.

ח אַל־תּוֹכַח לֵץ פֶּן־יִשְׂנָאֶךָּ הוֹכַח לְחָכָם וְיֶאֱהָבֶךָּ:

⁹ Instruct a wise man, and he will grow wiser; Teach a righteous man, and he will gain in learning.

ט תֵּן לְחָכָם וְיֶחְכַּם־עוֹד הוֹדַע לְצַדִּיק וְיוֹסֶף לֶקַח:

¹⁰ The beginning of wisdom is fear of *Hashem*, And knowledge of the Holy One is understanding.

י תְּחִלַּת חָכְמָה יִרְאַת יְהֹוָה וְדַעַת קְדֹשִׁים בִּינָה:

¹¹ For through me your days will increase, And years be added to your life.

יא כִּי־בִי יִרְבּוּ יָמֶיךָ וְיוֹסִיפוּ לְּךָ שְׁנוֹת חַיִּים:

¹² If you are wise, you are wise for yourself; If you are a scoffer, you bear it alone.

יב אִם־חָכַמְתָּ חָכַמְתָּ לָּךְ וְלַצְתָּ לְבַדְּךָ תִשָּׂא:

¹³ The stupid woman bustles about; She is simple and knows nothing.

יג אֵשֶׁת כְּסִילוּת הֹמִיָּה פְּתַיּוּת וּבַל־יָדְעָה מָּה:

¹⁴ She sits in the doorway of her house, Or on a chair at the heights of the town,

יד וְיָשְׁבָה לְפֶתַח בֵּיתָהּ עַל־כִּסֵּא מְרֹמֵי קָרֶת:

---

* clauses transposed for clarity

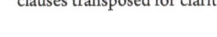

9:1 She has hewn her seven pillars The number seven is a recurring motif in the Bible, typically representing nature. It is used in the book of *Mishlei* as a way of expressing multitudes, so here it means wisdom has many pillars. According to the medieval commentator *Rashi*, in this context the number seven represents the seven days of creation. When *Hashem* created the world, the "house" referred to in the first half of this verse, He created it with wisdom.

Pillars in the ancient city of *Beit She'an*

15

15 Calling to all the wayfarers Who go about their own affairs,

טו לִקְרֹא לְעֹבְרֵי־דָרֶךְ הַמְיַשְּׁרִים אֹרְחוֹתָם:

16 "Let the simple enter here"; And to those devoid of sense she says,

טז מִי־פֶתִי יָסֻר הֵנָּה וַחֲסַר־לֵב וְאָמְרָה לּוֹ:

17 "Stolen waters are sweet, And bread eaten furtively is tasty."

יז מַיִם־גְּנוּבִים יִמְתָּקוּ וְלֶחֶם סְתָרִים יִנְעָם:

18 He does not know that the shades are there, That her guests are in the depths of Sheol.

יח וְלֹא־יָדַע כִּי־רְפָאִים שָׁם בְּעִמְקֵי שְׁאוֹל קְרֻאֶיהָ:

10 1 The proverbs of *Shlomo*: A wise son brings joy to his father; A dull son is his mother's sorrow.

י א מִשְׁלֵי שְׁלֹמֹה בֵּן חָכָם יְשַׂמַּח־אָב וּבֵן כְּסִיל תּוּגַת אִמּוֹ:

2 Ill-gotten wealth is of no avail, But righteousness saves from death.

ב לֹא־יוֹעִילוּ אוֹצְרוֹת רֶשַׁע וּצְדָקָה תַּצִּיל מִמָּוֶת:

3 *Hashem* will not let the righteous go hungry, But He denies the wicked what they crave.

ג לֹא־יַרְעִיב יְהוָה נֶפֶשׁ צַדִּיק וְהַוַּת רְשָׁעִים יֶהְדֹּף:

4 Negligent hands cause poverty, But diligent hands enrich.

ד רָאשׁ עֹשֶׂה כַף־רְמִיָּה וְיַד חָרוּצִים תַּעֲשִׁיר:

5 He who lays in stores during the summer is a capable son, But he who sleeps during the harvest is an incompetent.

ה אֹגֵר בַּקַּיִץ בֵּן מַשְׂכִּיל נִרְדָּם בַּקָּצִיר בֵּן מֵבִישׁ:

6 Blessings light upon the head of the righteous, But lawlessness covers the mouth of the wicked.

ו בְּרָכוֹת לְרֹאשׁ צַדִּיק וּפִי רְשָׁעִים יְכַסֶּה חָמָס:

7 The name of the righteous is invoked in blessing, But the fame of the wicked rots.

ז זֵכֶר צַדִּיק לִבְרָכָה וְשֵׁם רְשָׁעִים יִרְקָב:

8 He whose heart is wise accepts commands, But he whose speech is foolish comes to grief.

ח חֲכַם־לֵב יִקַּח מִצְוֹת וֶאֱוִיל שְׂפָתַיִם יִלָּבֵט:

9 He who lives blamelessly lives safely, But he who walks a crooked path will be found out.

ט הוֹלֵךְ בַּתֹּם יֵלֶךְ בֶּטַח וּמְעַקֵּשׁ דְּרָכָיו יִוָּדֵעַ:

10 He who winks his eye causes sorrow; He whose speech is foolish comes to grief.

י קֹרֵץ עַיִן יִתֵּן עַצָּבֶת וֶאֱוִיל שְׂפָתַיִם יִלָּבֵט:

11 The mouth of the righteous is a fountain of life, But lawlessness covers the mouth of the wicked.

יא מְקוֹר חַיִּים פִּי צַדִּיק וּפִי רְשָׁעִים יְכַסֶּה חָמָס:

12 Hatred stirs up strife, But love covers up all faults.

יב שִׂנְאָה תְּעוֹרֵר מְדָנִים וְעַל כָּל־פְּשָׁעִים תְּכַסֶּה אַהֲבָה:

13 Wisdom is to be found on the lips of the intelligent, But a rod is ready for the back of the senseless.

יג בְּשִׂפְתֵי נָבוֹן תִּמָּצֵא חָכְמָה וְשֵׁבֶט לְגֵו חֲסַר־לֵב:

14 The wise store up knowledge; The mouth of the fool is an imminent ruin.

יד חֲכָמִים יִצְפְּנוּ־דָעַת וּפִי־אֱוִיל מְחִתָּה קְרֹבָה:

15 The wealth of a rich man is his fortress; The poverty of the poor is his ruin.

טו הוֹן עָשִׁיר קִרְיַת עֻזּוֹ מְחִתַּת דַּלִּים רֵישָׁם:

16 The labor of the righteous man makes for life; The produce of the wicked man makes for want.

טז פְּעֻלַּת צַדִּיק לְחַיִּים תְּבוּאַת רָשָׁע לְחַטָּאת:

¹⁷ He who follows discipline shows the way to life, But he who ignores reproof leads astray.

יז אֹרַח לְחַיִּים שׁוֹמֵר מוּסָר וְעוֹזֵב תּוֹכַחַת מַתְעֶה:

¹⁸ He who conceals hatred has lying lips, While he who speaks forth slander is a dullard.

יח מְכַסֶּה שִׂנְאָה שִׂפְתֵי־שָׁקֶר וּמוֹצִא דִבָּה הוּא כְסִיל:

¹⁹ Where there is much talking, there is no lack of transgressing, But he who curbs his tongue shows sense.

יט בְּרֹב דְּבָרִים לֹא יֶחְדַּל־פָּשַׁע וְחֹשֵׂךְ שְׂפָתָיו מַשְׂכִּיל:

²⁰ The tongue of a righteous man is choice silver, But the mind of the wicked is of little worth.

כ כֶּסֶף נִבְחָר לְשׁוֹן צַדִּיק לֵב רְשָׁעִים כִּמְעָט:

²¹ The lips of the righteous sustain many, But fools die for lack of sense.

כא שִׂפְתֵי צַדִּיק יִרְעוּ רַבִּים וֶאֱוִילִים בַּחֲסַר־לֵב יָמוּתוּ:

²² It is the blessing of *Hashem* that enriches, And no toil can increase it.

כב בִּרְכַּת יְהֹוָה הִיא תַעֲשִׁיר וְלֹא־יוֹסִף עֶצֶב עִמָּהּ:

bir-KAT a-do-NAI HEE ta-a-SHEER v'-LO yo-SIF E-tzev i-MAH

²³ As mischief is sport for the dullard, So is wisdom for the man of understanding.

כג כִּשְׂחוֹק לִכְסִיל עֲשׂוֹת זִמָּה וְחָכְמָה לְאִישׁ תְּבוּנָה:

²⁴ What the wicked man plots overtakes him; What the righteous desire is granted.

כד מְגוֹרַת רָשָׁע הִיא תְבוֹאֶנּוּ וְתַאֲוַת צַדִּיקִים יִתֵּן:

²⁵ When the storm passes the wicked man is gone, But the righteous is an everlasting foundation.

כה כַּעֲבוֹר סוּפָה וְאֵין רָשָׁע וְצַדִּיק יְסוֹד עוֹלָם:

²⁶ Like vinegar to the teeth, Like smoke to the eyes, Is a lazy man to those who send him on a mission.

כו כַּחֹמֶץ לַשִּׁנַּיִם וְכֶעָשָׁן לָעֵינָיִם כֵּן הֶעָצֵל לְשֹׁלְחָיו:

²⁷ The fear of *Hashem* prolongs life, While the years of the wicked will be shortened.

כז יִרְאַת יְהֹוָה תּוֹסִיף יָמִים וּשְׁנוֹת רְשָׁעִים תִּקְצֹרְנָה:

²⁸ The righteous can look forward to joy, But the hope of the wicked is doomed.

כח תּוֹחֶלֶת צַדִּיקִים שִׂמְחָה וְתִקְוַת רְשָׁעִים תֹּאבֵד:

²⁹ The way of *Hashem* is a stronghold for the blameless, But a ruin for evildoers.

כט מָעוֹז לַתֹּם דֶּרֶךְ יְהֹוָה וּמְחִתָּה לְפֹעֲלֵי אָוֶן:

³⁰ The righteous will never be shaken; The wicked will not inhabit the earth.

ל צַדִּיק לְעוֹלָם בַּל־יִמּוֹט וּרְשָׁעִים לֹא יִשְׁכְּנוּ־אָרֶץ:

10:22 It is the blessing of *Hashem* that enriches In *Sefer Devarim* (11:10–12), the *Torah* describes how the Promised Land is different from Egypt. In Egypt, one could water his crops from the Nile by using his foot to easily direct water to his fields, but in the Land of Israel, the eyes of *Hashem* are on the land. It is only through His blessings, as our verse says, that the land enriches and provides its fruits. Modern Israel has compensated for its lack of natural water resources and limited rainfall through great technological breakthroughs such as water recycling and desalination. Nevertheless, we must always remember that even with great technology and innovation, "it is the blessing of *Hashem* that enriches."

Granot water desalination plant

Proverbs

משלי
פרק יא

³¹ The mouth of the righteous produces wisdom, But the treacherous tongue shall be cut off.

לא פִּי־צַדִּיק יָנוּב חָכְמָה וּלְשׁוֹן תַּהְפֻּכוֹת תִּכָּרֵת:

³² The lips of the righteous know what is pleasing; The mouth of the wicked [knows] duplicity.

לב שִׂפְתֵי צַדִּיק יֵדְעוּן רָצוֹן וּפִי רְשָׁעִים תַּהְפֻּכוֹת:

11 ¹ False scales are an abomination to *Hashem*; An honest weight pleases Him.

יא א מֹאזְנֵי מִרְמָה תּוֹעֲבַת יְהֹוָה וְאֶבֶן שְׁלֵמָה רְצוֹנוֹ:

² When arrogance appears, disgrace follows, But wisdom is with those who are unassuming.

ב בָּא־זָדוֹן וַיָּבֹא קָלוֹן וְאֶת־צְנוּעִים חָכְמָה:

³ The integrity of the upright guides them; The deviousness of the treacherous leads them to ruin.

ג תֻּמַּת יְשָׁרִים תַּנְחֵם וְסֶלֶף בּוֹגְדִים ושדם [וְשַׁדָּם:]

⁴ Wealth is of no avail on the day of wrath, But righteousness saves from death.

ד לֹא־יוֹעִיל הוֹן בְּיוֹם עֶבְרָה וּצְדָקָה תַּצִּיל מִמָּוֶת:

⁵ The righteousness of the blameless man smooths his way, But the wicked man is felled by his wickedness.

ה צִדְקַת תָּמִים תְּיַשֵּׁר דַּרְכּוֹ וּבְרִשְׁעָתוֹ יִפֹּל רָשָׁע:

⁶ The righteousness of the upright saves them, But the treacherous are trapped by their malice.

ו צִדְקַת יְשָׁרִים תַּצִּילֵם וּבְהַוַּת בֹּגְדִים יִלָּכֵדוּ:

⁷ At death the hopes of a wicked man are doomed, And the ambition of evil men comes to nothing.

ז בְּמוֹת אָדָם רָשָׁע תֹּאבַד תִּקְוָה וְתוֹחֶלֶת אוֹנִים אָבָדָה:

⁸ The righteous man is rescued from trouble And the wicked man takes his place.

ח צַדִּיק מִצָּרָה נֶחֱלָץ וַיָּבֹא רָשָׁע תַּחְתָּיו:

⁹ The impious man destroys his neighbor through speech, But through their knowledge the righteous are rescued.

ט בְּפֶה חָנֵף יַשְׁחִת רֵעֵהוּ וּבְדַעַת צַדִּיקִים יֵחָלֵצוּ:

¹⁰ When the righteous prosper the city exults; When the wicked perish there are shouts of joy.

י בְּטוּב צַדִּיקִים תַּעֲלֹץ קִרְיָה וּבַאֲבֹד רְשָׁעִים רִנָּה:

¹¹ A city is built up by the blessing of the upright, But it is torn down by the speech of the wicked.

יא בְּבִרְכַּת יְשָׁרִים תָּרוּם קָרֶת וּבְפִי רְשָׁעִים תֵּהָרֵס:

¹² He who speaks contemptuously of his fellowman is devoid of sense; A prudent man keeps his peace.

יב בָּז־לְרֵעֵהוּ חֲסַר־לֵב וְאִישׁ תְּבוּנוֹת יַחֲרִישׁ:

¹³ A base fellow gives away secrets, But a trustworthy soul keeps a confidence.

יג הוֹלֵךְ רָכִיל מְגַלֶּה־סּוֹד וְנֶאֱמַן־רוּחַ מְכַסֶּה דָבָר:

¹⁴ For want of strategy an army falls, But victory comes with much planning.

יד בְּאֵין תַּחְבֻּלוֹת יִפָּל־עָם וּתְשׁוּעָה בְּרֹב יוֹעֵץ:

¹⁵ Harm awaits him who stands surety for another; He who spurns pledging shall be secure.

טו רַע־יֵרוֹעַ כִּי־עָרַב זָר וְשֹׂנֵא תֹקְעִים בּוֹטֵחַ:

¹⁶ A graceful woman obtains honor; Ruthless men obtain wealth.

טז אֵשֶׁת־חֵן תִּתְמֹךְ כָּבוֹד וְעָרִיצִים יִתְמְכוּ־עֹשֶׁר:

17 A kindly man benefits himself; A cruel man makes trouble for himself.

גֹּמֵל נַפְשׁוֹ אִישׁ חָסֶד וְעֹכֵר שְׁאֵרוֹ אַכְזָרִי:

18 The wicked man earns illusory wages, But he who sows righteousness has a true reward.

רָשָׁע עֹשֶׂה פְעֻלַּת־שָׁקֶר וְזֹרֵעַ צְדָקָה שֶׂכֶר אֱמֶת:

19 Righteousness is a prop of life, But to pursue evil leads to death.

כֵּן־צְדָקָה לְחַיִּים וּמְרַדֵּף רָעָה לְמוֹתוֹ:

20 Men of crooked mind are an abomination to *Hashem*, But those whose way is blameless please Him.

תּוֹעֲבַת יְהוָֹה עִקְּשֵׁי־לֵב וּרְצוֹנוֹ תְּמִימֵי דָרֶךְ:

21 Assuredly, the evil man will not escape, But the offspring of the righteous will be safe.

יָד לְיָד לֹא־יִנָּקֶה רָּע וְזֶרַע צַדִּיקִים נִמְלָט:

22 Like a gold ring in the snout of a pig Is a beautiful woman bereft of sense.

נֶזֶם זָהָב בְּאַף חֲזִיר אִשָּׁה יָפָה וְסָרַת טָעַם:

23 What the righteous desire can only be good; What the wicked hope for [stirs] wrath.

תַּאֲוַת צַדִּיקִים אַךְ־טוֹב תִּקְוַת רְשָׁעִים עֶבְרָה:

24 One man gives generously and ends with more; Another stints on doing the right thing and incurs a loss.

יֵשׁ מְפַזֵּר וְנוֹסָף עוֹד וְחוֹשֵׂךְ מִיֹּשֶׁר אַךְ־לְמַחְסוֹר:

25 A generous person enjoys prosperity; He who satisfies others shall himself be sated.

נֶפֶשׁ־בְּרָכָה תְדֻשָּׁן וּמַרְוֶה גַּם־הוּא יוֹרֶא:

26 He who withholds grain earns the curses of the people, But blessings are on the head of the one who dispenses it.

מֹנֵעַ בָּר יִקְּבֻהוּ לְאוֹם וּבְרָכָה לְרֹאשׁ מַשְׁבִּיר:

mo-NAY-a BAR yi-k'-VU-hu l'-OM uv-ra-KHAH l'-ROSH mash-BEER

27 He who earnestly seeks what is good pursues what is pleasing; He who is bent on evil, upon him it shall come.

שֹׁחֵר טוֹב יְבַקֵּשׁ רָצוֹן וְדֹרֵשׁ רָעָה תְבוֹאֶנּוּ:

28 He who trusts in his wealth shall fall, But the righteous shall flourish like foliage.

בּוֹטֵחַ בְּעָשְׁרוֹ הוּא יִפֹּל וְכֶעָלֶה צַדִּיקִים יִפְרָחוּ:

29 He who makes trouble for his household shall inherit the wind; A fool is a slave to the wise-hearted.

עוֹכֵר בֵּיתוֹ יִנְחַל־רוּחַ וְעֶבֶד אֱוִיל לַחֲכַם־לֵב:

A lettuce field in the Sharon region of Israel

11:26 He who withholds grain earns the curses of the people The Bible commands the Israelites to set aside a certain portion of their crops, grown in the Land of Israel, for the poor. The corners of their fields, the forgotten sheaves and the grains that fall during harvest are all to be left for the needy (Leviticus 19:9–10, Deuteronomy 24:19). In *Megillat Rut*, *Boaz* sustains his community in this manner and *Rut*, the poor widow, gathers in his field (chapter 2). This biblical imperative is still practiced in Israel today. Each season, farmers throughout Israel leave over millions of pounds of produce from their fields, which are collected by volunteers and distributed to poor people all over the country.

30 The fruit of the righteous is a tree of life; A wise man captivates people.

ל פְּרִי־צַדִּיק עֵץ חַיִּים וְלֹקֵחַ נְפָשׁוֹת חָכָם:

31 If the righteous on earth get their deserts, How much more the wicked man and the sinner.

לא הֵן צַדִּיק בָּאָרֶץ יְשֻׁלָּם אַף כִּי־רָשָׁע וְחוֹטֵא:

12 1 He who loves discipline loves knowledge; He who spurns reproof is a brutish man.

יב א אֹהֵב מוּסָר אֹהֵב דָּעַת וְשֹׂנֵא תוֹכַחַת בָּעַר:

2 A good man earns the favor of *Hashem*, A man of intrigues, His condemnation.

ב טוֹב יָפִיק רָצוֹן מֵיהֹוָה וְאִישׁ מְזִמּוֹת יַרְשִׁיעַ:

3 A man cannot be established in wickedness, But the root of the righteous will not be shaken loose.

ג לֹא־יִכּוֹן אָדָם בְּרֶשַׁע וְשֹׁרֶשׁ צַדִּיקִים בַּל־יִמּוֹט:

4 A capable wife is a crown for her husband, But an incompetent one is like rot in his bones.

ד אֵשֶׁת־חַיִל עֲטֶרֶת בַּעְלָהּ וּכְרָקָב בְּעַצְמוֹתָיו מְבִישָׁה:

5 The purposes of the righteous are justice, The schemes of the wicked are deceit.

ה מַחְשְׁבוֹת צַדִּיקִים מִשְׁפָּט תַּחְבֻּלוֹת רְשָׁעִים מִרְמָה:

6 The words of the wicked are a deadly ambush, But the speech of the upright saves them.

ו דִּבְרֵי רְשָׁעִים אֱרָב־דָּם וּפִי יְשָׁרִים יַצִּילֵם:

7 Overturn the wicked and they are gone, But the house of the righteous will endure.

ז הָפוֹךְ רְשָׁעִים וְאֵינָם וּבֵית צַדִּיקִים יַעֲמֹד:

8 A man is commended according to his intelligence; A twisted mind is held up to contempt.

ח לְפִי־שִׂכְלוֹ יְהֻלַּל־אִישׁ וְנַעֲוֵה־לֵב יִהְיֶה לָבוּז:

9 Better to be lightly esteemed and have a servant Than to put on airs and have no food.

ט טוֹב נִקְלֶה וְעֶבֶד לוֹ מִמְּתַכַּבֵּד וַחֲסַר־לָחֶם:

10 A righteous man knows the needs of his beast, But the compassion of the wicked is cruelty.

י יוֹדֵעַ צַדִּיק נֶפֶשׁ בְּהֶמְתּוֹ וְרַחֲמֵי רְשָׁעִים אַכְזָרִי:

11 He who tills his land shall have food in plenty, But he who pursues vanities is devoid of sense.

יא עֹבֵד אַדְמָתוֹ יִשְׂבַּע־לָחֶם וּמְרַדֵּף רֵיקִים חֲסַר־לֵב:

o-VAYD ad-ma-TO yis-ba LA-chem um-ra-DAYF ray-KEEM cha-sar LAYV

12 The wicked covet the catch of evil men; The root of the righteous yields [fruit].

יב חָמַד רָשָׁע מְצוֹד רָעִים וְשֹׁרֶשׁ צַדִּיקִים יִתֵּן:

13 Sinful speech is a trap for the evil man, But the righteous escapes from trouble.

יג בְּפֶשַׁע שְׂפָתַיִם מוֹקֵשׁ רָע וַיֵּצֵא מִצָּרָה צַדִּיק:

14 A man gets his fill of good from the fruit of his speech; One is repaid in kind for one's deeds.

יד מִפְּרִי פִי־אִישׁ יִשְׂבַּע־טוֹב וּגְמוּל יְדֵי־אָדָם ישוב [יָשִׁיב] לוֹ:

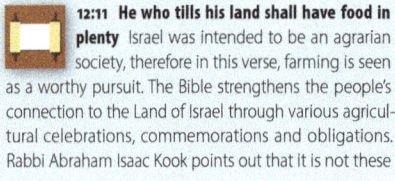

12:11 He who tills his land shall have food in plenty Israel was intended to be an agrarian society, therefore in this verse, farming is seen as a worthy pursuit. The Bible strengthens the people's connection to the Land of Israel through various agricultural celebrations, commemorations and obligations. Rabbi Abraham Isaac Kook points out that it is not these laws, unique to *Eretz Yisrael*, which make the land holy. Rather, it is the intrinsic holiness of the land that inspires these special agricultural commandments.

An Israeli farmer looks out on his field during the Sabbatical year

Proverbs

15 The way of a fool is right in his own eyes; But the wise man accepts advice.

טו דֶּרֶךְ אֱוִיל יָשָׁר בְּעֵינָיו וְשֹׁמֵעַ לְעֵצָה חָכָם:

16 A fool's vexation is known at once, But a clever man conceals his humiliation.

טז אֱוִיל בַּיּוֹם יִוָּדַע כַּעְסוֹ וְכֹסֶה קָלוֹן עָרוּם:

17 He who testifies faithfully tells the truth, But a false witness, deceit.

יז יָפִיחַ אֱמוּנָה יַגִּיד צֶדֶק וְעֵד שְׁקָרִים מִרְמָה:

18 There is blunt talk like sword-thrusts, But the speech of the wise is healing.

יח יֵשׁ בּוֹטֶה כְּמַדְקְרוֹת חָרֶב וּלְשׁוֹן חֲכָמִים מַרְפֵּא:

19 Truthful speech abides forever, A lying tongue for but a moment.

יט שְׂפַת־אֱמֶת תִּכּוֹן לָעַד וְעַד־אַרְגִּיעָה לְשׁוֹן שָׁקֶר:

20 Deceit is in the minds of those who plot evil; For those who plan good there is joy.

כ מִרְמָה בְּלֶב־חֹרְשֵׁי רָע וּלְיֹעֲצֵי שָׁלוֹם שִׂמְחָה:

21 No harm befalls the righteous, But the wicked have their fill of misfortune.

כא לֹא־יְאֻנֶּה לַצַּדִּיק כָּל־אָוֶן וּרְשָׁעִים מָלְאוּ רָע:

22 Lying speech is an abomination to *Hashem*, But those who act faithfully please Him.

כב תּוֹעֲבַת יְהֹוָה שִׂפְתֵי־שָׁקֶר וְעֹשֵׂי אֱמוּנָה רְצוֹנוֹ:

23 A clever man conceals what he knows, But the mind of a dullard cries out folly.

כג אָדָם עָרוּם כֹּסֶה דָּעַת וְלֵב כְּסִילִים יִקְרָא אִוֶּלֶת:

24 The hand of the diligent wields authority; The negligent are held in subjection.

כד יַד־חָרוּצִים תִּמְשׁוֹל וּרְמִיָּה תִּהְיֶה לָמַס:

25 If there is anxiety in a man's mind let him quash it, And turn it into joy with a good word.

כה דְּאָגָה בְלֶב־אִישׁ יַשְׁחֶנָּה וְדָבָר טוֹב יְשַׂמְּחֶנָּה:

26 A righteous man gives his friend direction, But the way of the wicked leads astray.

כו יָתֵר מֵרֵעֵהוּ צַדִּיק וְדֶרֶךְ רְשָׁעִים תַּתְעֵם:

27 A negligent man never has game to roast; A diligent man has precious wealth.

כז לֹא־יַחֲרֹךְ רְמִיָּה צֵידוֹ וְהוֹן־אָדָם יָקָר חָרוּץ:

28 The road of righteousness leads to life; By way of its path there is no death.

כח בְּאֹרַח־צְדָקָה חַיִּים וְדֶרֶךְ נְתִיבָה אַל־מָוֶת:

13 1 A wise son – it is through the discipline of his father; A scoffer – he never heard reproof.

יג א בֵּן חָכָם מוּסַר אָב וְלֵץ לֹא־שָׁמַע גְּעָרָה:

2 A man enjoys good from the fruit of his speech; But out of the throat of the treacherous comes lawlessness.

ב מִפְּרִי פִי־אִישׁ יֹאכַל טוֹב וְנֶפֶשׁ בֹּגְדִים חָמָס:

3 He who guards his tongue preserves his life; He who opens wide his lips, it is his ruin.

ג נֹצֵר פִּיו שֹׁמֵר נַפְשׁוֹ פֹּשֵׂק שְׂפָתָיו מְחִתָּה־לוֹ:

4 A lazy man craves, but has nothing; The diligent shall feast on rich fare.

ד מִתְאַוָּה וָאַיִן נַפְשׁוֹ עָצֵל וְנֶפֶשׁ חָרֻצִים תְּדֻשָּׁן:

5 A righteous man hates lies; The wicked man is vile and disgraceful.

ה דְּבַר־שֶׁקֶר יִשְׂנָא צַדִּיק וְרָשָׁע יַבְאִישׁ וְיַחְפִּיר׃

6 Righteousness protects him whose way is blameless; Wickedness subverts the sinner.

ו צְדָקָה תִּצֹּר תָּם־דָּרֶךְ וְרִשְׁעָה תְּסַלֵּף חַטָּאת׃

7 One man pretends to be rich and has nothing; Another professes to be poor and has much wealth.

ז יֵשׁ מִתְעַשֵּׁר וְאֵין כֹּל מִתְרוֹשֵׁשׁ וְהוֹן רָב׃

8 Riches are ransom for a man's life, The poor never heard a reproof.

ח כֹּפֶר נֶפֶשׁ־אִישׁ עָשְׁרוֹ וְרָשׁ לֹא־שָׁמַע גְּעָרָה׃

9 The light of the righteous is radiant; The lamp of the wicked is extinguished.

ט אוֹר־צַדִּיקִים יִשְׂמָח וְנֵר רְשָׁעִים יִדְעָךְ׃

10 Arrogance yields nothing but strife; Wisdom belongs to those who seek advice.

י רַק־בְּזָדוֹן יִתֵּן מַצָּה וְאֶת־נוֹעָצִים חָכְמָה׃

11 Wealth may dwindle to less than nothing, But he who gathers little by little increases it.

יא הוֹן מֵהֶבֶל יִמְעָט וְקֹבֵץ עַל־יָד יַרְבֶּה׃

12 Hope deferred sickens the heart, But desire realized is a tree of life.

יב תּוֹחֶלֶת מְמֻשָּׁכָה מַחֲלָה־לֵב וְעֵץ חַיִּים תַּאֲוָה בָאָה׃

13 He who disdains a precept will be injured thereby; He who respects a command will be rewarded.

יג בָּז לְדָבָר יֵחָבֶל לוֹ וִירֵא מִצְוָה הוּא יְשֻׁלָּם׃

14 The instruction of a wise man is a fountain of life, Enabling one to avoid deadly snares.

יד תּוֹרַת חָכָם מְקוֹר חַיִּים לָסוּר מִמֹּקְשֵׁי מָוֶת׃

15 Good sense wins favor; The way of treacherous men is unchanging.

טו שֵׂכֶל־טוֹב יִתֶּן־חֵן וְדֶרֶךְ בֹּגְדִים אֵיתָן׃

16 Every clever man acts knowledgeably, But a dullard exposes his stupidity.

טז כָּל־עָרוּם יַעֲשֶׂה בְדָעַת וּכְסִיל יִפְרֹשׂ אִוֶּלֶת׃

17 Harm befalls a wicked messenger; A faithful courier brings healing.

יז מַלְאָךְ רָשָׁע יִפֹּל בְּרָע וְצִיר אֱמוּנִים מַרְפֵּא׃

18 Poverty and humiliation are for him who spurns discipline; But he who takes reproof to heart gets honor.

יח רֵישׁ וְקָלוֹן פּוֹרֵעַ מוּסָר וְשׁוֹמֵר תּוֹכַחַת יְכֻבָּד׃

19 Desire realized is sweet to the soul; To turn away from evil is abhorrent to the stupid.

יט תַּאֲוָה נִהְיָה תֶּעֱרַב לְנָפֶשׁ וְתוֹעֲבַת כְּסִילִים סוּר מֵרָע׃

20 He who keeps company with the wise becomes wise, But he who consorts with dullards comes to grief.

כ הלוך [הוֹלֵךְ] אֶת־חֲכָמִים וחכם [יֶחְכָּם] וְרֹעֶה כְסִילִים יֵרוֹעַ׃

21 Misfortune pursues sinners, But the righteous are well rewarded.

כא חַטָּאִים תְּרַדֵּף רָעָה וְאֶת־צַדִּיקִים יְשַׁלֶּם־טוֹב׃

22 A good man has what to bequeath to his grandchildren, For the wealth of sinners is stored up for the righteous.

כב טוֹב יַנְחִיל בְּנֵי־בָנִים וְצָפוּן לַצַּדִּיק חֵיל חוֹטֵא:

TOV yan-KHEEL b'-nay va-NEEM v'-tza-FUN la-tza-DEEK KHAYL kho-TAY

23 The tillage of the poor yields much food; But substance is swept away for lack of moderation.

כג רָב־אֹכֶל נִיר רָאשִׁים וְיֵשׁ נִסְפֶּה בְּלֹא מִשְׁפָּט:

24 He who spares the rod hates his son, But he who loves him disciplines him early.

כד חוֹשֵׂךְ שִׁבְטוֹ שׂוֹנֵא בְנוֹ וְאֹהֲבוֹ שִׁחֲרוֹ מוּסָר:

25 The righteous man eats to his heart's content, But the belly of the wicked is empty.

כה צַדִּיק אֹכֵל לְשֹׂבַע נַפְשׁוֹ וּבֶטֶן רְשָׁעִים תֶּחְסָר:

14 1 The wisest of women builds her house, But folly tears it down with its own hands.

יד א חַכְמוֹת נָשִׁים בָּנְתָה בֵיתָהּ וְאִוֶּלֶת בְּיָדֶיהָ תֶהֶרְסֶנּוּ:

2 He who maintains his integrity fears *Hashem*; A man of devious ways scorns Him.

ב הוֹלֵךְ בְּיָשְׁרוֹ יְרֵא יְהוָה וּנְלוֹז דְּרָכָיו בּוֹזֵהוּ:

3 In the mouth of a fool is a rod of haughtiness, But the lips of the wise protect them.

ג בְּפִי־אֱוִיל חֹטֶר גַּאֲוָה וְשִׂפְתֵי חֲכָמִים תִּשְׁמוּרֵם:

4 If there are no oxen the crib is clean, But a rich harvest comes through the strength of the ox.

ד בְּאֵין אֲלָפִים אֵבוּס בָּר וְרָב־תְּבוּאוֹת בְּכֹחַ שׁוֹר:

5 An honest witness will not lie; A false witness testifies lies.

ה עֵד אֱמוּנִים לֹא יְכַזֵּב וְיָפִיחַ כְּזָבִים עֵד שָׁקֶר:

6 A scoffer seeks wisdom in vain, But knowledge comes easily to the intelligent man.

ו בִּקֶּשׁ־לֵץ חָכְמָה וָאָיִן וְדַעַת לְנָבוֹן נָקָל:

7 Keep your distance from a dullard, For you will not learn wise speech.

ז לֵךְ מִנֶּגֶד לְאִישׁ כְּסִיל וּבַל־יָדַעְתָּ שִׂפְתֵי־דָעַת:

8 It is the wisdom of a clever man to understand his course; But the stupidity of the dullard is delusion.

ח חָכְמַת עָרוּם הָבִין דַּרְכּוֹ וְאִוֶּלֶת כְּסִילִים מִרְמָה:

9 Reparations mediate between fools, Between the upright, good will.

ט אֱוִלִים יָלִיץ אָשָׁם וּבֵין יְשָׁרִים רָצוֹן:

10 The heart alone knows its bitterness, And no outsider can share in its joy.

י לֵב יוֹדֵעַ מָרַּת נַפְשׁוֹ וּבְשִׂמְחָתוֹ לֹא־יִתְעָרַב זָר:

11 The house of the wicked will be demolished, But the tent of the upright will flourish.

יא בֵּית רְשָׁעִים יִשָּׁמֵד וְאֹהֶל יְשָׁרִים יַפְרִיחַ:

Grandparents and grandchildren with the *Chanukkah menorah*

13:22 A good man has what to bequeath to his grandchildren A righteous man leaves more than a physical inheritance for his children and grandchildren, as the merit of his good deeds is also bequeathed to them. By contrast, though, the sinner's wealth will ultimately pass to more worthy hands. The greatest inheritance left to the Jewish people is the Land of Israel, not to be squandered or given away, but passed to down to their children's children for eternity.

Proverbs

¹² A road may seem right to a man, But in the end it is a road to death.

יב יֵשׁ דֶּרֶךְ יָשָׁר לִפְנֵי־אִישׁ וְאַחֲרִיתָהּ דַּרְכֵי־מָוֶת:

¹³ The heart may ache even in laughter, And joy may end in grief.

יג גַּם־בִּשְׂחֹק יִכְאַב־לֵב וְאַחֲרִיתָהּ שִׂמְחָה תוּגָה:

¹⁴ An unprincipled man reaps the fruits of his ways; A good man, of his deeds.

יד מִדְּרָכָיו יִשְׂבַּע סוּג לֵב וּמֵעָלָיו אִישׁ טוֹב:

¹⁵ A simple person believes anything; A clever man ponders his course.

טו פֶּתִי יַאֲמִין לְכָל־דָּבָר וְעָרוּם יָבִין לַאֲשֻׁרוֹ:

¹⁶ A wise man is diffident and shuns evil, But a dullard rushes in confidently.

טז חָכָם יָרֵא וְסָר מֵרָע וּכְסִיל מִתְעַבֵּר וּבוֹטֵחַ:

¹⁷ An impatient man commits folly; A man of intrigues will be hated.

יז קְצַר־אַפַּיִם יַעֲשֶׂה אִוֶּלֶת וְאִישׁ מְזִמּוֹת יִשָּׂנֵא:

¹⁸ Folly is the lot of the simple, But clever men glory in knowledge.

יח נָחֲלוּ פְתָאיִם אִוֶּלֶת וַעֲרוּמִים יַכְתִּרוּ דָעַת:

¹⁹ Evil men are brought low before the good, So are the wicked at the gates of the righteous.

יט שַׁחוּ רָעִים לִפְנֵי טוֹבִים וּרְשָׁעִים עַל־שַׁעֲרֵי צַדִּיק:

²⁰ A pauper is despised even by his peers, But a rich man has many friends.

כ גַּם־לְרֵעֵהוּ יִשָּׂנֵא רָשׁ וְאֹהֲבֵי עָשִׁיר רַבִּים:

²¹ He who despises his fellow is wrong; He who shows pity for the lowly is happy.

כא בָּז־לְרֵעֵהוּ חוֹטֵא וּמְחוֹנֵן עֲנִיִּים [עֲנָוִים] אַשְׁרָיו:

²² Surely those who plan evil go astray, While those who plan good earn steadfast love.

כב הֲלוֹא־יִתְעוּ חֹרְשֵׁי רָע וְחֶסֶד וֶאֱמֶת חֹרְשֵׁי טוֹב:

²³ From all toil there is some gain, But idle chatter is pure loss.

כג בְּכָל־עֶצֶב יִהְיֶה מוֹתָר וּדְבַר־שְׂפָתַיִם אַךְ־לְמַחְסוֹר:

²⁴ The ornament of the wise is their wealth; The stupidity of dullards is stupidity.

כד עֲטֶרֶת חֲכָמִים עָשְׁרָם אִוֶּלֶת כְּסִילִים אִוֶּלֶת:

²⁵ A truthful witness saves lives; He who testifies lies [spreads] deceit.

כה מַצִּיל נְפָשׁוֹת עֵד אֱמֶת וְיָפִחַ כְּזָבִים מִרְמָה:

²⁶ Fear of *Hashem* is a stronghold, A refuge for a man's children.

כו בְּיִרְאַת יְהֹוָה מִבְטַח־עֹז וּלְבָנָיו יִהְיֶה מַחְסֶה:

²⁷ Fear of *Hashem* is a fountain of life, Enabling one to avoid deadly snares.

כז יִרְאַת יְהֹוָה מְקוֹר חַיִּים לָסוּר מִמֹּקְשֵׁי מָוֶת:

²⁸ A numerous people is the glory of a king; Without a nation a ruler is ruined.

כח בְּרָב־עָם הַדְרַת־מֶלֶךְ וּבְאֶפֶס לְאֹם מְחִתַּת רָזוֹן:

b'-rov AM had-rat ME-lekh uv-E-fes l'-OM m'-khi-TAT ra-ZON

 14:28 A numerous people is the glory of a king
This verse is frequently understood in reference to *Hashem* Himself. His glory is increased when the multitudes of His people follow His ways, bringing Him a good name in the eyes of the world. Based on this verse, Jewish tradition teaches that if a person has a

Proverbs

29 Patience results in much understanding; Impatience gets folly as its portion.

כט אֶרֶךְ אַפַּיִם רַב־תְּבוּנָה וּקְצַר־רוּחַ מֵרִים אִוֶּלֶת:

30 A calm disposition gives bodily health; Passion is rot to the bones.

ל מְאוֹר־עֵינַיִם יְשַׂמַּח־לֵב מַרְפֵּא לֵב וּרְקַב עֲצָמוֹת קִנְאָה:

31 He who withholds what is due to the poor affronts his Maker; He who shows pity for the needy honors Him.

לא עֹשֵׁק־דָּל חֵרֵף עֹשֵׂהוּ וּמְכַבְּדוֹ חֹנֵן אֶבְיוֹן:

32 The wicked man is felled by his own evil; The righteous man finds security in his death.

לב בְּרָעָתוֹ יִדָּחֶה רָשָׁע וְחֹסֶה בְמוֹתוֹ צַדִּיק:

33 Wisdom rests quietly in the mind of a prudent man, But among dullards it makes itself known.

לג בְּלֵב נָבוֹן תָּנוּחַ חָכְמָה וּבְקֶרֶב כְּסִילִים תִּוָּדֵעַ:

34 Righteousness exalts a nation; Sin is a reproach to any people.

לד צְדָקָה תְרוֹמֵם־גּוֹי וְחֶסֶד לְאֻמִּים חַטָּאת:

35 The king favors a capable servant; He rages at an incompetent one.

לה רְצוֹן־מֶלֶךְ לְעֶבֶד מַשְׂכִּיל וְעֶבְרָתוֹ תִּהְיֶה מֵבִישׁ:

15 1 A gentle response allays wrath; A harsh word provokes anger.

טו א מַעֲנֶה־רַּךְ יָשִׁיב חֵמָה וּדְבַר־עֶצֶב יַעֲלֶה־אָף:

2 The tongue of the wise produces much knowledge, But the mouth of dullards pours out folly.

ב לְשׁוֹן חֲכָמִים תֵּיטִיב דָּעַת וּפִי כְסִילִים יַבִּיעַ אִוֶּלֶת:

3 The eyes of *Hashem* are everywhere, Observing the bad and the good.

ג בְּכָל־מָקוֹם עֵינֵי יְהֹוָה צֹפוֹת רָעִים וְטוֹבִים:

4 A healing tongue is a tree of life, But a devious one makes for a broken spirit.

ד מַרְפֵּא לָשׁוֹן עֵץ חַיִּים וְסֶלֶף בָּהּ שֶׁבֶר בְּרוּחַ:

5 A fool spurns the discipline of his father, But one who heeds reproof becomes clever.

ה אֱוִיל יִנְאַץ מוּסַר אָבִיו וְשֹׁמֵר תּוֹכַחַת יַעְרִם:

6 In the house of the righteous there is much treasure, But in the harvest of the wicked there is trouble.

ו בֵּית צַדִּיק חֹסֶן רָב וּבִתְבוּאַת רָשָׁע נֶעְכָּרֶת:

7 The lips of the wise disseminate knowledge; Not so the minds of dullards.

ז שִׂפְתֵי חֲכָמִים יְזָרוּ דָעַת וְלֵב כְּסִילִים לֹא־כֵן:

8 The sacrifice of the wicked is an abomination to *Hashem*, But the prayer of the upright pleases Him.

ח זֶבַח רְשָׁעִים תּוֹעֲבַת יְהֹוָה וּתְפִלַּת יְשָׁרִים רְצוֹנוֹ:

Rabbi Tuly Weisz and his family greeting new immigrants to Israel

choice of houses of worship in which he could pray, it is preferable to worship God in the larger congregation, for "A numerous people is the glory of a king." The ultimate expression of God's glory, however, can be learned from its inverse: The greatest disgrace to *Hashem*'s glory is when the Children of Israel are isolated, scattered and exiled from the land. The greatest glory to the King of Kings, therefore, is the return of the People of Israel to the Land of Israel in large numbers. How fortunate is our generation that has seen millions of Jews from the four corners of the world return *en masse* to live in Israel, thereby bringing glory to the King of Kings.

9 The way of the wicked is an abomination to *Hashem*, But He loves him who pursues righteousness.

ט תּוֹעֲבַת יְהֹוָה דֶּרֶךְ רָשָׁע וּמְרַדֵּף צְדָקָה יֶאֱהָב:

10 Discipline seems bad to him who forsakes the way; He who spurns reproof will die.

י מוּסָר רָע לְעֹזֵב אֹרַח שׂוֹנֵא תוֹכַחַת יָמוּת:

11 Sheol and Abaddon lie exposed to *Hashem*, How much more the minds of men!

יא שְׁאוֹל וַאֲבַדּוֹן נֶגֶד יְהֹוָה אַף כִּי־לִבּוֹת בְּנֵי־אָדָם:

12 The scoffer dislikes being reproved; He will not resort to the wise.

יב לֹא יֶאֱהַב־לֵץ הוֹכֵחַ לוֹ אֶל־חֲכָמִים לֹא יֵלֵךְ:

13 A joyful heart makes a cheerful face; A sad heart makes a despondent mood.

יג לֵב שָׂמֵחַ יֵיטִב פָּנִים וּבְעַצְּבַת־לֵב רוּחַ נְכֵאָה:

14 The mind of a prudent man seeks knowledge; The mouth of the dullard pursues folly.

יד לֵב נָבוֹן יְבַקֶּשׁ־דָּעַת וּפְנֵי [וּפִי] כְסִילִים יִרְעֶה אִוֶּלֶת:

15 All the days of a poor man are wretched, But contentment is a feast without end.

טו כָּל־יְמֵי עָנִי רָעִים וְטוֹב־לֵב מִשְׁתֶּה תָמִיד:

16 Better a little with fear of *Hashem* Than great wealth with confusion.

טז טוֹב־מְעַט בְּיִרְאַת יְהֹוָה מֵאוֹצָר רָב וּמְהוּמָה בוֹ:

tov m'-AT b'-yir-AT a-do-NAI may-o-TZAR RAV um-HU-mah VO

17 Better a meal of vegetables where there is love Than a fattened ox where there is hate.

יז טוֹב אֲרֻחַת יָרָק וְאַהֲבָה־שָׁם מִשּׁוֹר אָבוּס וְשִׂנְאָה־בוֹ:

18 A hot-tempered man provokes a quarrel; A patient man calms strife.

יח אִישׁ חֵמָה יְגָרֶה מָדוֹן וְאֶרֶךְ אַפַּיִם יַשְׁקִיט רִיב:

19 The way of a lazy man is like a hedge of thorns, But the path of the upright is paved.

יט דֶּרֶךְ עָצֵל כִּמְשֻׂכַת חָדֶק וְאֹרַח יְשָׁרִים סְלֻלָה:

20 A wise son makes his father happy; A fool of a man humiliates his mother.

כ בֵּן חָכָם יְשַׂמַּח־אָב וּכְסִיל אָדָם בּוֹזֶה אִמּוֹ:

21 Folly is joy to one devoid of sense; A prudent man walks a straight path.

כא אִוֶּלֶת שִׂמְחָה לַחֲסַר־לֵב וְאִישׁ תְּבוּנָה יְיַשֶּׁר־לָכֶת:

22 Plans are foiled for want of counsel, But they succeed through many advisers.

כב הָפֵר מַחֲשָׁבוֹת בְּאֵין סוֹד וּבְרֹב יוֹעֲצִים תָּקוּם:

23 A ready response is a joy to a man, And how good is a word rightly timed!

כג שִׂמְחָה לָאִישׁ בְּמַעֲנֵה־פִיו וְדָבָר בְּעִתּוֹ מַה־טּוֹב:

A modest street in Safed, Israel

15:16 Better a little with fear of *Hashem* *Shlomo* presents the reader an understanding of true value. It is better to have only a little, accompanied by faith in *Hashem*, than to have much wealth, but suffer from inner turmoil and doubt. This eternal truth is especially evident in today's celebrity culture, where so many people who seem to have it all suffer publicly from depression and family insta-bility. In contrast to the constant and empty pursuit of fame and fortune, King *Shlomo* teaches "better a little with fear of *Hashem.*"

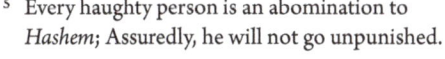

²⁴ For an intelligent man the path of life leads upward, In order to avoid Sheol below.

כד אֹרַח חַיִּים לְמַעְלָה לְמַשְׂכִּיל לְמַעַן סוּר מִשְּׁאוֹל מָטָּה:

²⁵ *Hashem* will tear down the house of the proud, But He will establish the homestead of the widow.

כה בֵּית גֵּאִים יִסַּח יְהֹוָה וְיַצֵּב גְּבוּל אַלְמָנָה:

²⁶ Evil thoughts are an abomination to *Hashem*, But pleasant words are pure.

כו תּוֹעֲבַת יְהֹוָה מַחְשְׁבוֹת רָע וּטְהֹרִים אִמְרֵי־נֹעַם:

²⁷ He who pursues ill-gotten gain makes trouble for his household; He who spurns gifts will live long.

כז עֹכֵר בֵּיתוֹ בּוֹצֵעַ בָּצַע וְשׂוֹנֵא מַתָּנֹת יִחְיֶה:

²⁸ The heart of the righteous man rehearses his answer, But the mouth of the wicked blurts out evil things.

כח לֵב צַדִּיק יֶהְגֶּה לַעֲנוֹת וּפִי רְשָׁעִים יַבִּיעַ רָעוֹת:

²⁹ *Hashem* is far from the wicked, But He hears the prayer of the righteous.

כט רָחוֹק יְהֹוָה מֵרְשָׁעִים וּתְפִלַּת צַדִּיקִים יִשְׁמָע:

³⁰ What brightens the eye gladdens the heart; Good news puts fat on the bones.

ל מְאוֹר־עֵינַיִם יְשַׂמַּח־לֵב שְׁמוּעָה טוֹבָה תְּדַשֶּׁן־עָצֶם:

³¹ He whose ear heeds the discipline of life Lodges among the wise.

לא אֹזֶן שֹׁמַעַת תּוֹכַחַת חַיִּים בְּקֶרֶב חֲכָמִים תָּלִין:

³² He who spurns discipline hates himself; He who heeds reproof gains understanding.

לב פּוֹרֵעַ מוּסָר מֹאֵס נַפְשׁוֹ וְשׁוֹמֵעַ תּוֹכַחַת קוֹנֶה לֵּב:

³³ The fear of *Hashem* is the discipline of wisdom; Humility precedes honor.

לג יִרְאַת יְהֹוָה מוּסַר חָכְמָה וְלִפְנֵי כָבוֹד עֲנָוָה:

16 ¹ A man may arrange his thoughts, But what he says depends on *Hashem*.

טז א לְאָדָם מַעַרְכֵי־לֵב וּמֵיְהֹוָה מַעֲנֵה לָשׁוֹן:

² All the ways of a man seem right to him, But *Hashem* probes motives.

ב כָּל־דַּרְכֵי־אִישׁ זַךְ בְּעֵינָיו וְתֹכֵן רוּחוֹת יְהֹוָה:

³ Entrust your affairs to *Hashem*, And your plans will succeed.

ג גֹּל אֶל־יְהֹוָה מַעֲשֶׂיךָ וְיִכֹּנוּ מַחְשְׁבֹתֶיךָ:

⁴ *Hashem* made everything for a purpose, Even the wicked for an evil day.

ד כֹּל פָּעַל יְהֹוָה לַמַּעֲנֵהוּ וְגַם־רָשָׁע לְיוֹם רָעָה:

KOL pa-AL a-do-NAI l'-ma-a-NAY-hu v'-gam ra-SHA l'-YOM ra-AH

⁵ Every haughty person is an abomination to *Hashem*; Assuredly, he will not go unpunished.

ה תּוֹעֲבַת יְהֹוָה כָּל־גְּבַהּ־לֵב יָד לְיָד לֹא יִנָּקֶה:

Israeli child in a wheat field wrapped in an Israeli flag

16:4 *Hashem* made everything for a purpose Since we know that *Hashem* is good, sometimes we assume that bad things happen despite Him. This verse reminds us that everything, even that which we perceive as evil, was created by God for a purpose. Though the reason is not always clear, we must look for the good that comes from every situation. The slavery in Egypt, for example, led to the formation of the Nation of Israel, the giving of the Torah on Mount Sinai, and ultimately the acquisition of the Land of Israel. With this verse in mind, we can rest assured that Israel's many enemies and the threats facing the Jewish state today are also part of *Hashem*'s divine plan and will lead to the greatest good: The redemption of Israel and the world.

Proverbs

6 Iniquity is expiated by loyalty and faithfulness, And evil is avoided through fear of *Hashem*.

ו בְּחֶסֶד וֶאֱמֶת יְכֻפַּר עָוֺן וּבְיִרְאַת יְהוָה סוּר מֵרָע:

7 When *Hashem* is pleased with a man's conduct, He may turn even his enemies into allies.

ז בִּרְצוֹת יְהוָה דַּרְכֵי־אִישׁ גַּם־אוֹיְבָיו יַשְׁלִם אִתּוֹ:

8 Better a little with righteousness Than a large income with injustice.

ח טוֹב־מְעַט בִּצְדָקָה מֵרֹב תְּבוּאוֹת בְּלֹא מִשְׁפָּט:

9 A man may plot out his course, But it is *Hashem* who directs his steps.

ט לֵב אָדָם יְחַשֵּׁב דַּרְכּוֹ וַיהוָה יָכִין צַעֲדוֹ:

10 There is magic on the lips of the king; He cannot err in judgment.

י קֶסֶם עַל־שִׂפְתֵי־מֶלֶךְ בְּמִשְׁפָּט לֹא יִמְעַל־פִּיו:

11 Honest scales and balances are *Hashem's*; All the weights in the bag are His work.

יא פֶּלֶס וּמֹאזְנֵי מִשְׁפָּט לַיהוָה מַעֲשֵׂהוּ כָּל־אַבְנֵי־כִיס:

12 Wicked deeds are an abomination to kings, For the throne is established by righteousness.

יב תּוֹעֲבַת מְלָכִים עֲשׂוֹת רֶשַׁע כִּי בִצְדָקָה יִכּוֹן כִּסֵּא:

13 Truthful speech wins the favor of kings; They love those who speak honestly.

יג רְצוֹן מְלָכִים שִׂפְתֵי־צֶדֶק וְדֹבֵר יְשָׁרִים יֶאֱהָב:

14 The king's wrath is a messenger of death, But a wise man can appease it.

יד חֲמַת־מֶלֶךְ מַלְאֲכֵי־מָוֶת וְאִישׁ חָכָם יְכַפְּרֶנָּה:

15 The king's smile means life; His favor is like a rain cloud in spring.

טו בְּאוֹר־פְּנֵי־מֶלֶךְ חַיִּים וּרְצוֹנוֹ כְּעָב מַלְקוֹשׁ:

16 How much better to acquire wisdom than gold; To acquire understanding is preferable to silver.

טז קְנֹה־חָכְמָה מַה־טּוֹב מֵחָרוּץ וּקְנוֹת בִּינָה נִבְחָר מִכָּסֶף:

17 The highway of the upright avoids evil; He who would preserve his life watches his way.

יז מְסִלַּת יְשָׁרִים סוּר מֵרָע שֹׁמֵר נַפְשׁוֹ נֹצֵר דַּרְכּוֹ:

18 Pride goes before ruin, Arrogance, before failure.

יח לִפְנֵי־שֶׁבֶר גָּאוֹן וְלִפְנֵי כִשָּׁלוֹן גֹּבַהּ רוּחַ:

19 Better to be humble and among the lowly Than to share spoils with the proud.

יט טוֹב שְׁפַל־רוּחַ אֶת־עניים [עֲנָוִים] מֵחַלֵּק שָׁלָל אֶת־גֵּאִים:

20 He who is adept in a matter will attain success; Happy is he who trusts in *Hashem*.

כ מַשְׂכִּיל עַל־דָּבָר יִמְצָא־טוֹב וּבוֹטֵחַ בַּיהוָה אַשְׁרָיו:

21 The wise-hearted is called discerning; One whose speech is pleasing gains wisdom.

כא לַחֲכַם־לֵב יִקָּרֵא נָבוֹן וּמֶתֶק שְׂפָתַיִם יֹסִיף לֶקַח:

22 Good sense is a fountain of life to those who have it, And folly is the punishment of fools.

כב מְקוֹר חַיִּים שֵׂכֶל בְּעָלָיו וּמוּסַר אֱוִלִים אִוֶּלֶת:

23 The mind of the wise man makes his speech effective And increases the wisdom on his lips.

כג לֵב חָכָם יַשְׂכִּיל פִּיהוּ וְעַל־שְׂפָתָיו יֹסִיף לֶקַח:

24 Pleasant words are like a honeycomb, Sweet to the palate and a cure for the body.

כד צוּף־דְּבַשׁ אִמְרֵי־נֹעַם מָתוֹק לַנֶּפֶשׁ וּמַרְפֵּא לָעָצֶם:

25 A road may seem right to a man, But in the end it is a road to death.

כה יֵשׁ דֶּרֶךְ יָשָׁר לִפְנֵי־אִישׁ וְאַחֲרִיתָהּ דַּרְכֵי־מָוֶת:

26 The appetite of a laborer labors for him, Because his hunger forces him on.

כו נֶפֶשׁ עָמֵל עָמְלָה לּוֹ כִּי־אָכַף עָלָיו פִּיהוּ:

27 A scoundrel plots evil; What is on his lips is like a scorching fire.

כז אִישׁ בְּלִיַּעַל כֹּרֶה רָעָה וְעַל־שְׂפָתָיו [שְׂפָתוֹ] כְּאֵשׁ צָרָבֶת:

28 A shifty man stirs up strife, And a querulous one alienates his friend.

כח אִישׁ תַּהְפֻּכוֹת יְשַׁלַּח מָדוֹן וְנִרְגָּן מַפְרִיד אַלּוּף:

29 A lawless man misleads his friend, Making him take the wrong way.

כט אִישׁ חָמָס יְפַתֶּה רֵעֵהוּ וְהוֹלִיכוֹ בְּדֶרֶךְ לֹא־טוֹב:

30 He closes his eyes while meditating deception; He purses his lips while deciding upon evil.

ל עֹצֶה עֵינָיו לַחְשֹׁב תַּהְפֻּכוֹת קֹרֵץ שְׂפָתָיו כִּלָּה רָעָה:

31 Gray hair is a crown of glory; It is attained by the way of righteousness.

לא עֲטֶרֶת תִּפְאֶרֶת שֵׂיבָה בְּדֶרֶךְ צְדָקָה תִּמָּצֵא:

32 Better to be forbearing than mighty, To have self-control than to conquer a city.

לב טוֹב אֶרֶךְ אַפַּיִם מִגִּבּוֹר וּמֹשֵׁל בְּרוּחוֹ מִלֹּכֵד עִיר:

33 Lots are cast into the lap; The decision depends on *Hashem*.

לג בַּחֵיק יוּטַל אֶת־הַגּוֹרָל וּמֵיהֹוָה כָּל־מִשְׁפָּטוֹ:

17 1 Better a dry crust with peace Than a house full of feasting with strife.

יז א טוֹב פַּת חֲרֵבָה וְשַׁלְוָה־בָהּ מִבַּיִת מָלֵא זִבְחֵי־רִיב:

2 A capable servant will dominate an incompetent son And share the inheritance with the brothers.

ב עֶבֶד־מַשְׂכִּיל יִמְשֹׁל בְּבֵן מֵבִישׁ וּבְתוֹךְ אַחִים יַחֲלֹק נַחֲלָה:

3 For silver – the crucible; For gold – the furnace, And *Hashem* tests the mind.

ג מַצְרֵף לַכֶּסֶף וְכוּר לַזָּהָב וּבֹחֵן לִבּוֹת יְהֹוָה:

4 An evildoer listens to mischievous talk; A liar gives ear to malicious words.

ד מֵרַע מַקְשִׁיב עַל־שְׂפַת־אָוֶן שֶׁקֶר מֵזִין עַל־לְשׁוֹן הַוֹּת:

5 He who mocks the poor affronts his Maker; He who rejoices over another's misfortune will not go unpunished.

ה לֹעֵג לָרָשׁ חֵרֵף עֹשֵׂהוּ שָׂמֵחַ לְאֵיד לֹא יִנָּקֶה:

6 Grandchildren are the crown of their elders, And the glory of children is their parents.

ו עֲטֶרֶת זְקֵנִים בְּנֵי בָנִים וְתִפְאֶרֶת בָּנִים אֲבוֹתָם:

a-TE-ret z'-kay-NEEM b'-NAY va-NEEM v'-tif-E-ret ba-NEEM a-vo-TAM

17:6 Grandchildren are the crown of their elders This verse extols the blessing of grandchildren, much like the passage in *Sefer Tehillim* (128:6). In *Sefer Tehillim*, however, the blessing of grandchildren is couched between references to the well-being of *Yerushalayim* and *Eretz Yisrael*: "May you share the prosperity of *Yerushalayim* all the days of your life, and live to see your children's children. May all be well with *Yisrael* (literally, 'may peace be upon *Yisrael*')" (Psalms 128:5–6). What is the connection between children's children and the welfare of *Eretz Yisrael* and *Yerushalayim*? It has been suggested that verse 5 should be understood as a com- mand rather than a promise: See the good of Jerusalem. We must empha- size and talk about what is special and precious about the Land of Israel, in- stead of complaining and focusing on the negative. If that is how we relate to land, and that is what we convey and pass down to our children and grandchildren, then there is a hope for a future in which peace will be upon Israel.

A grandfather and his grandson appreciating the beauty of the Land of Israel

Proverbs

7 Lofty words are not fitting for a villain; Much less lying words for a great man.

ז לֹא־נָאוָה לְנָבָל שְׂפַת־יֶתֶר אַף כִּי־לְנָדִיב שְׂפַת־שָׁקֶר:

8 A bribe seems like a charm to him who uses it; He succeeds at every turn.

ח אֶבֶן־חֵן הַשֹּׁחַד בְּעֵינֵי בְעָלָיו אֶל־כָּל־אֲשֶׁר יִפְנֶה יַשְׂכִּיל:

9 He who seeks love overlooks faults, But he who harps on a matter alienates his friend.

ט מְכַסֶּה־פֶּשַׁע מְבַקֵּשׁ אַהֲבָה וְשֹׁנֶה בְדָבָר מַפְרִיד אַלּוּף:

10 A rebuke works on an intelligent man More than one hundred blows on a fool.

י תֵּחַת גְּעָרָה בְמֵבִין מֵהַכּוֹת כְּסִיל מֵאָה:

11 An evil man seeks only to rebel; A ruthless messenger will be sent against him.

יא אַךְ־מְרִי יְבַקֶּשׁ־רָע וּמַלְאָךְ אַכְזָרִי יְשֻׁלַּח־בּוֹ:

12 Sooner meet a bereaved she-bear Than a fool with his nonsense.

יב פָּגוֹשׁ דֹּב שַׁכּוּל בְּאִישׁ וְאַל־כְּסִיל בְּאִוַּלְתּוֹ:

13 Evil will never depart from the house Of him who repays good with evil.

יג מֵשִׁיב רָעָה תַּחַת טוֹבָה לֹא־תמיש [תָמוּשׁ] רָעָה מִבֵּיתוֹ:

14 To start a quarrel is to open a sluice; Before a dispute flares up, drop it.

יד פּוֹטֵר מַיִם רֵאשִׁית מָדוֹן וְלִפְנֵי הִתְגַּלַּע הָרִיב נְטוֹשׁ:

15 To acquit the guilty and convict the innocent – Both are an abomination to *Hashem*.

טו מַצְדִּיק רָשָׁע וּמַרְשִׁיעַ צַדִּיק תּוֹעֲבַת יְהֹוָה גַּם־שְׁנֵיהֶם:

16 What good is money in the hand of a fool To purchase wisdom, when he has no mind?

טז לָמָּה־זֶּה מְחִיר בְּיַד־כְּסִיל לִקְנוֹת חָכְמָה וְלֶב־אָיִן:

17 A friend is devoted at all times; A brother is born to share adversity.

יז בְּכָל־עֵת אֹהֵב הָרֵעַ וְאָח לְצָרָה יִוָּלֵד:

18 Devoid of sense is he who gives his hand To stand surety for his fellow.

יח אָדָם חֲסַר־לֵב תּוֹקֵעַ כָּף עֹרֵב עֲרֻבָּה לִפְנֵי רֵעֵהוּ:

19 He who loves transgression loves strife; He who builds a high threshold invites broken bones.

יט אֹהֵב פֶּשַׁע אֹהֵב מַצָּה מַגְבִּיהַּ פִּתְחוֹ מְבַקֶּשׁ־שָׁבֶר:

20 Man of crooked mind comes to no good, And he who speaks duplicity falls into trouble.

כ עִקֶּשׁ־לֵב לֹא יִמְצָא־טוֹב וְנֶהְפָּךְ בִּלְשׁוֹנוֹ יִפּוֹל בְּרָעָה:

21 One begets a dullard to one's own grief; The father of a villain has no joy.

כא יֹלֵד כְּסִיל לְתוּגָה לוֹ וְלֹא־יִשְׂמַח אֲבִי נָבָל:

22 A joyful heart makes for good health; Despondency dries up the bones.

כב לֵב שָׂמֵחַ יֵיטִב גֵּהָה וְרוּחַ נְכֵאָה תְּיַבֶּשׁ־גָּרֶם:

23 The wicked man draws a bribe out of his bosom To pervert the course of justice.

כג שֹׁחַד מֵחֵיק רָשָׁע יִקָּח לְהַטּוֹת אָרְחוֹת מִשְׁפָּט:

24 Wisdom lies before the intelligent man; The eyes of the dullard range to the ends of the earth.

כד אֶת־פְּנֵי מֵבִין חָכְמָה וְעֵינֵי כְסִיל בִּקְצֵה־אָרֶץ:

25 A stupid son is vexation for his father And a heartache for the woman who bore him.

כה כַּעַס לְאָבִיו בֵּן כְּסִיל וּמֶמֶר לְיוֹלַדְתּוֹ:

²⁶ To punish the innocent is surely not right, Or to flog the great for their uprightness.

גַּם עֲנוֹשׁ לַצַּדִּיק לֹא־טוֹב לְהַכּוֹת נְדִיבִים עַל־יֹשֶׁר: כו

²⁷ A knowledgeable man is sparing with his words; A man of understanding is reticent.

חוֹשֵׂךְ אֲמָרָיו יוֹדֵעַ דָּעַת וקר־[יְקַר־] רוּחַ אִישׁ תְּבוּנָה: כז

²⁸ Even a fool, if he keeps silent, is deemed wise; Intelligent, if he seals his lips.

גַּם אֱוִיל מַחֲרִישׁ חָכָם יֵחָשֵׁב אֹטֵם שְׂפָתָיו נָבוֹן: כח

18 ¹ He who isolates himself pursues his desires; He disdains all competence.

לְתַאֲוָה יְבַקֵּשׁ נִפְרָד בְּכָל־תּוּשִׁיָּה יִתְגַּלָּע: א **ח**

² The fool does not desire understanding, But only to air his thoughts.

לֹא־יַחְפֹּץ כְּסִיל בִּתְבוּנָה כִּי אִם־בְּהִתְגַּלּוֹת לִבּוֹ: ב

³ Comes the wicked man comes derision, And with the rogue, contempt.

בְּבוֹא־רָשָׁע בָּא גַם־בּוּז וְעִם־קָלוֹן חֶרְפָּה: ג

⁴ The words a man speaks are deep waters, A flowing stream, a fountain of wisdom.

מַיִם עֲמֻקִּים דִּבְרֵי פִי־אִישׁ נַחַל נֹבֵעַ מְקוֹר חָכְמָה: ד

⁵ It is not right to be partial to the guilty And subvert the innocent in judgment.

שְׂאֵת פְּנֵי־רָשָׁע לֹא־טוֹב לְהַטּוֹת צַדִּיק בַּמִּשְׁפָּט: ה

⁶ The words of a fool lead to strife; His speech invites blows.

שִׂפְתֵי כְסִיל יָבֹאוּ בְרִיב וּפִיו לְמַהֲלֻמוֹת יִקְרָא: ו

⁷ The fool's speech is his ruin; His words are a trap for him.

פִּי־כְסִיל מְחִתָּה־לוֹ וּשְׂפָתָיו מוֹקֵשׁ נַפְשׁוֹ: ז

⁸ The words of a querulous man are bruising; They penetrate one's inmost parts.

דִּבְרֵי נִרְגָּן כְּמִתְלַהֲמִים וְהֵם יָרְדוּ חַדְרֵי־בָטֶן: ח

⁹ One who is slack in his work Is a brother to a vandal.

גַּם מִתְרַפֶּה בִמְלַאכְתּוֹ אָח הוּא לְבַעַל מַשְׁחִית: ט

¹⁰ The name of *Hashem* is a tower of strength To which the righteous man runs and is safe.

מִגְדַּל־עֹז שֵׁם יְהוָה בּוֹ־יָרוּץ צַדִּיק וְנִשְׂגָּב: י

¹¹ The wealth of a rich man is his fortress; In his fancy it is a protective wall.

הוֹן עָשִׁיר קִרְיַת עֻזּוֹ וּכְחוֹמָה נִשְׂגָּבָה בְּמַשְׂכִּיתוֹ: יא

¹² Before ruin a man's heart is proud; Humility goes before honor.

לִפְנֵי־שֶׁבֶר יִגְבַּהּ לֵב־אִישׁ וְלִפְנֵי כָבוֹד עֲנָוָה: יב

¹³ To answer a man before hearing him out Is foolish and disgraceful.

מֵשִׁיב דָּבָר בְּטֶרֶם יִשְׁמָע אִוֶּלֶת הִיא־לוֹ וּכְלִמָּה: יג

¹⁴ A man's spirit can sustain him through illness; But low spirits – who can bear them?

רוּחַ־אִישׁ יְכַלְכֵּל מַחֲלֵהוּ וְרוּחַ נְכֵאָה מִי יִשָּׂאֶנָּה: יד

¹⁵ The mind of an intelligent man acquires knowledge; The ears of the wise seek out knowledge.

לֵב נָבוֹן יִקְנֶה־דָּעַת וְאֹזֶן חֲכָמִים תְּבַקֶּשׁ־דָּעַת: טו

¹⁶ A man's gift eases his way And gives him access to the great.

מַתָּן אָדָם יַרְחִיב לוֹ וְלִפְנֵי גְדֹלִים יַנְחֶנּוּ: טז

17 The first to plead his case seems right Till the other party examines him.

צַדִּיק הָרִאשׁוֹן בְּרִיבוֹ יבא־[וּבָא־] רֵעֵהוּ וַחֲקָרוֹ:

18 The lot puts an end to strife And separates those locked in dispute.

מִדְיָנִים יַשְׁבִּית הַגּוֹרָל וּבֵין עֲצוּמִים יַפְרִיד:

19 A brother offended is more formidable than a stronghold; Such strife is like the bars of a fortress.

אָח נִפְשָׁע מִקִּרְיַת־עֹז ומדונים [וּמִדְיָנִים] כִּבְרִיחַ אַרְמוֹן:

20 A man's belly is filled by the fruit of his mouth; He will be filled by the produce of his lips.

מִפְּרִי פִי־אִישׁ תִּשְׂבַּע בִּטְנוֹ תְּבוּאַת שְׂפָתָיו יִשְׂבָּע:

21 Death and life are in the power of the tongue; Those who love it will eat its fruit.

מָוֶת וְחַיִּים בְּיַד־לָשׁוֹן וְאֹהֲבֶיהָ יֹאכַל פִּרְיָהּ:

22 He who finds a wife has found happiness And has won the favor of *Hashem*.

מָצָא אִשָּׁה מָצָא טוֹב וַיָּפֶק רָצוֹן מֵיְהֹוָה:

ma-TZA i-SHAH MA-tza TOV va-YA-fek ra-TZON may-a-do-NAI

23 The poor man speaks beseechingly; The rich man's answer is harsh.

תַּחֲנוּנִים יְדַבֶּר־רָשׁ וְעָשִׁיר יַעֲנֶה עַזּוֹת:

24 There are companions to keep one company, And there is a friend more devoted than a brother.

אִישׁ רֵעִים לְהִתְרֹעֵעַ וְיֵשׁ אֹהֵב דָּבֵק מֵאָח:

19 1 Better a poor man who lives blamelessly Than one who speaks perversely and is a dullard.

יט טוֹב־רָשׁ הוֹלֵךְ בְּתֻמּוֹ מֵעִקֵּשׁ שְׂפָתָיו וְהוּא כְסִיל:

2 A person without knowledge is surely not good; He who moves hurriedly blunders.

גַּם בְּלֹא־דַעַת נֶפֶשׁ לֹא־טוֹב וְאָץ בְּרַגְלַיִם חוֹטֵא:

3 A man's folly subverts his way, And his heart rages against *Hashem*.

אִוֶּלֶת אָדָם תְּסַלֵּף דַּרְכּוֹ וְעַל־יְהֹוָה יִזְעַף לִבּוֹ:

4 Wealth makes many friends, But a poor man loses his last friend.

הוֹן יֹסִיף רֵעִים רַבִּים וְדָל מֵרֵעֵהוּ יִפָּרֵד:

5 A false witness will not go unpunished; He who testifies lies will not escape.

עֵד שְׁקָרִים לֹא יִנָּקֶה וְיָפִיחַ כְּזָבִים לֹא יִמָּלֵט:

6 Many court the favor of a great man, And all are the friends of a dispenser of gifts.

רַבִּים יְחַלּוּ פְנֵי־נָדִיב וְכָל־הָרֵעַ לְאִישׁ מַתָּן:

7 All the brothers of a poor man despise him; How much more is he shunned by his friends! He who pursues words – they are of no avail.

כָּל אֲחֵי־רָשׁ שְׂנֵאֻהוּ אַף כִּי מְרֵעֵהוּ רָחֲקוּ מִמֶּנּוּ מְרַדֵּף אֲמָרִים לא־[לוֹ־] הֵמָּה:

A groom puts a ring on his bride's finger at an Ultra-Orthodox wedding in Jerusalem

א **18:22 He who finds a wife has found happiness** This verse is a parallel to the verse in which *Hashem* says, "It is not good for man to be alone; I will make a fitting helper for him" (Genesis 2:18). God wants man to find a wife who will serve as his partner in life. When he does, *Hashem* will bless that union, as it fulfils His will. The

Hebrew word for 'man' is *eesh* (איש), and the word for 'woman' is *eeshah* (אשה). The two words share two out of three Hebrew letters, א and ש. The other two letters, י and ה, spell one of the names of God. The Sages (*Sotah* 17a) teach that when man and woman unite in marriage and work together, the presence of the Lord resides with them.

איש
אישה

Proverbs

8 He who acquires wisdom is his own best friend; He preserves understanding and attains happiness.

קֹנֶה־לֵּב אֹהֵב נַפְשׁוֹ שֹׁמֵר תְּבוּנָה לִמְצֹא־טוֹב: ח

9 A false witness will not go unpunished; He who testifies falsely is doomed.

עֵד שְׁקָרִים לֹא יִנָּקֶה וְיָפִיחַ כְּזָבִים יֹאבֵד: ט

10 Luxury is not fitting for a dullard, Much less that a servant rule over princes.

לֹא־נָאוֶה לִכְסִיל תַּעֲנוּג אַף כִּי־לְעֶבֶד מְשֹׁל בְּשָׂרִים: י

11 A man shows intelligence by his forebearance; It is his glory when he overlooks an offense.

שֵׂכֶל אָדָם הֶאֱרִיךְ אַפּוֹ וְתִפְאַרְתּוֹ עֲבֹר עַל־פָּשַׁע: יא

12 The rage of a king is like the roar of a lion; His favor is like dew upon the grass.

נַהַם כַּכְּפִיר זַעַף מֶלֶךְ וּכְטַל עַל־עֵשֶׂב רְצוֹנוֹ: יב

NA-ham ka-k'-FEER ZA-af ME-lekh ukh-TAL al AY-sev r'-tzo-NO

13 A stupid son is a calamity to his father; The nagging of a wife is like the endless dripping of water.

הַוֹּת לְאָבִיו בֵּן כְּסִיל וְדֶלֶף טֹרֵד מִדְיְנֵי אִשָּׁה: יג

14 Property and riches are bequeathed by fathers, But an efficient wife comes from *Hashem*.

בַּיִת וָהוֹן נַחֲלַת אָבוֹת וּמֵיְהֹוָה אִשָּׁה מַשְׂכָּלֶת: יד

15 Laziness induces sleep, And a negligent person will go hungry.

עַצְלָה תַּפִּיל תַּרְדֵּמָה וְנֶפֶשׁ רְמִיָּה תִרְעָב: טו

16 He who has regard for his life pays regard to commandments; He who is heedless of his ways will die.

שֹׁמֵר מִצְוָה שֹׁמֵר נַפְשׁוֹ בּוֹזֵה דְרָכָיו יומת [יָמוּת]: טז

17 He who is generous to the poor makes a loan to *Hashem*; He will repay him his due.

מַלְוֵה יְהֹוָה חוֹנֵן דָּל וּגְמֻלוֹ יְשַׁלֶּם־לוֹ: יז

18 Discipline your son while there is still hope, And do not set your heart on his destruction.

יַסֵּר בִּנְךָ כִּי־יֵשׁ תִּקְוָה וְאֶל־הֲמִיתוֹ אַל־תִּשָּׂא נַפְשֶׁךָ: יח

19 A hot-tempered man incurs punishment; If you try to save him you will only make it worse.

גֹּרל־[גְּדָל־] חֵמָה נֹשֵׂא עֹנֶשׁ כִּי אִם־תַּצִּיל וְעוֹד תּוֹסִף: יט

20 Listen to advice and accept discipline In order that you may be wise in the end.

שְׁמַע עֵצָה וְקַבֵּל מוּסָר לְמַעַן תֶּחְכַּם בְּאַחֲרִיתֶךָ: כ

21 Many designs are in a man's mind, But it is *Hashem*'s plan that is accomplished.

רַבּוֹת מַחֲשָׁבוֹת בְּלֶב־אִישׁ וַעֲצַת יְהֹוָה הִיא תָקוּם: כא

22 Greed is a reproach to a man; Better be poor than a liar.

תַּאֲוַת אָדָם חַסְדּוֹ וְטוֹב־רָשׁ מֵאִישׁ כָּזָב: כב

19:12 His favor is like dew upon the grass Often, when the Bible mentions a king, it is a metaphor for *Hashem* Himself. Here, God's anger is likened to a lion's roar. A roar is frightening, but serves as a warning to its prey that the lion is present, and clever prey can escape. So too, *Hashem*'s anger is intended to warn us to correct our ways before it is too late. His blessing, however, is like dew which nurtures the grass. Unlike rain, which is a blessing but can also be destructive, dew serves only to help the grass grow. Similarly, the Lord's favor serves only to nurture, not to harm us.

Morning dew near *Beit Shemesh*

23 He who fears *Hashem* earns life; He shall abide in contentment, Free from misfortune.

כג יִרְאַת יְהוָה לְחַיִּים וְשָׂבֵעַ יָלִין בַּל־יִפָּקֶד רָע׃

24 The lazy man buries his hand in the bowl; He will not even bring it to his mouth.

כד טָמַן עָצֵל יָדוֹ בַּצַּלָּחַת גַּם־אֶל־פִּיהוּ לֹא יְשִׁיבֶנָּה׃

25 Beat the scoffer and the simple will become clever; Reprove an intelligent man and he gains knowledge.

כה לֵץ תַּכֶּה וּפֶתִי יַעְרִם וְהוֹכִיחַ לְנָבוֹן יָבִין דָּעַת׃

26 A son who causes shame and disgrace Plunders his father, puts his mother to flight.

כו מְשַׁדֶּד־אָב יַבְרִיחַ אֵם בֵּן מֵבִישׁ וּמַחְפִּיר׃

27 My son, cease to stray from words of knowledge And receive discipline.

כז חֲדַל־בְּנִי לִשְׁמֹעַ מוּסָר לִשְׁגוֹת מֵאִמְרֵי־דָעַת׃

28 A malicious witness scoffs at justice, And the speech of the wicked conceals mischief.

כח עֵד בְּלִיַּעַל יָלִיץ מִשְׁפָּט וּפִי רְשָׁעִים יְבַלַּע־אָוֶן׃

29 Punishments are in store for scoffers And blows for the backs of dullards.

כט נָכוֹנוּ לַלֵּצִים שְׁפָטִים וּמַהֲלֻמוֹת לְגֵו כְּסִילִים׃

20 1 Wine is a scoffer, strong drink a roisterer; He who is muddled by them will not grow wise.

כ א לֵץ הַיַּיִן הֹמֶה שֵׁכָר וְכָל־שֹׁגֶה בּוֹ לֹא יֶחְכָּם׃

2 The terror of a king is like the roar of a lion; He who provokes his anger risks his life.

ב נַהַם כַּכְּפִיר אֵימַת מֶלֶךְ מִתְעַבְּרוֹ חוֹטֵא נַפְשׁוֹ׃

3 It is honorable for a man to desist from strife, But every fool becomes embroiled.

ג כָּבוֹד לָאִישׁ שֶׁבֶת מֵרִיב וְכָל־אֱוִיל יִתְגַּלָּע׃

4 In winter the lazy man does not plow; At harvesttime he seeks, and finds nothing.

ד מֵחֹרֶף עָצֵל לֹא־יַחֲרֹשׁ ישאל [וְשָׁאַל] בַּקָּצִיר וָאָיִן׃

5 The designs in a man's mind are deep waters But a man of understanding can draw them out.

ה מַיִם עֲמֻקִּים עֵצָה בְלֶב־אִישׁ וְאִישׁ תְּבוּנָה יִדְלֶנָּה׃

6 He calls many a man his loyal friend, But who can find a faithful man?

ו רָב־אָדָם יִקְרָא אִישׁ חַסְדּוֹ וְאִישׁ אֱמוּנִים מִי יִמְצָא׃

7 The righteous man lives blamelessly; Happy are his children who come after him.

ז מִתְהַלֵּךְ בְּתֻמּוֹ צַדִּיק אַשְׁרֵי בָנָיו אַחֲרָיו׃

8 The king seated on the throne of judgment Can winnow out all evil by his glance.

ח מֶלֶךְ יוֹשֵׁב עַל־כִּסֵּא־דִין מְזָרֶה בְעֵינָיו כָּל־רָע׃

9 Who can say, "I have cleansed my heart, I am purged of my sin"?

ט מִי־יֹאמַר זִכִּיתִי לִבִּי טָהַרְתִּי מֵחַטָּאתִי׃

10 False weights and false measures, Both are an abomination to *Hashem*.

י אֶבֶן וָאֶבֶן אֵיפָה וְאֵיפָה תּוֹעֲבַת יְהוָה גַּם־שְׁנֵיהֶם׃

11 A child may be dissembling in his behavior Even though his actions are blameless and proper.

יא גַּם בְּמַעֲלָלָיו יִתְנַכֶּר־נָעַר אִם־זַךְ וְאִם־יָשָׁר פָּעֳלוֹ׃

12 The ear that hears, the eye that sees – *Hashem* made them both.

יב אֹזֶן שֹׁמַעַת וְעַיִן רֹאָה יְהוָה עָשָׂה גַּם־שְׁנֵיהֶם׃

13 Do not love sleep lest you be impoverished; Keep your eyes open and you will have plenty of food.

יג אַל־תֶּאֱהַב שֵׁנָה פֶּן־תִּוָּרֵשׁ פְּקַח עֵינֶיךָ שְׂבַע־לָחֶם:

14 "Bad, bad," says the buyer, But having moved off, he congratulates himself.

יד רַע רַע יֹאמַר הַקּוֹנֶה וְאֹזֵל לוֹ אָז יִתְהַלָּל:

15 Gold is plentiful, jewels abundant, But wise speech is a precious object.

טו יֵשׁ זָהָב וְרָב־פְּנִינִים וּכְלִי יְקָר שִׂפְתֵי־דָעַת:

16 Seize his garment, for he stood surety for another; Take it as a pledge, [for he stood surety] for an unfamiliar woman.

טז לְקַח־בִּגְדוֹ כִּי־עָרַב זָר וּבְעַד נכרים [נָכְרִיָּה] חַבְלֵהוּ:

17 Bread gained by fraud may be tasty to a man, But later his mouth will be filled with gravel.

יז עָרֵב לָאִישׁ לֶחֶם שָׁקֶר וְאַחַר יִמָּלֵא־פִיהוּ חָצָץ:

18 Plans laid in council will succeed; Wage war with stratagems.

יח מַחֲשָׁבוֹת בְּעֵצָה תִכּוֹן וּבְתַחְבֻּלוֹת עֲשֵׂה מִלְחָמָה:

19 He who gives away secrets is a base fellow; Do not take up with a garrulous man.

יט גּוֹלֶה־סּוֹד הוֹלֵךְ רָכִיל וּלְפֹתֶה שְׂפָתָיו לֹא תִתְעָרָב:

20 One who reviles his father or mother, Light will fail him when darkness comes.

כ מְקַלֵּל אָבִיו וְאִמּוֹ יִדְעַךְ נֵרוֹ באישון [בֶּאֱשׁוּן] חֹשֶׁךְ:

21 An estate acquired in haste at the outset Will not be blessed in the end.

כא נַחֲלָה מבחלת [מְבֹהֶלֶת] בָּרִאשֹׁנָה וְאַחֲרִיתָהּ לֹא תְבֹרָךְ:

22 Do not say, "I will requite evil"; Put your hope in *Hashem* and He will deliver you.

כב אַל־תֹּאמַר אֲשַׁלְּמָה־רָע קַוֵּה לַיהוָה וְיֹשַׁע לָךְ:

al to-MAR a-sha-l'-mah RA ka-VAY la-do-NAI v'-YO-sha LAKH

23 False weights are an abomination to *Hashem*; Dishonest scales are not right.

כג תּוֹעֲבַת יְהוָה אֶבֶן וָאָבֶן וּמֹאזְנֵי מִרְמָה לֹא־טוֹב:

24 A man's steps are decided by *Hashem*; What does a man know about his own way?

כד מֵיהוָה מִצְעֲדֵי־גָבֶר וְאָדָם מַה־יָּבִין דַּרְכּוֹ:

25 It is a snare for a man to pledge a sacred gift rashly And to give thought to his vows only after they have been made.

כה מוֹקֵשׁ אָדָם יָלַע קֹדֶשׁ וְאַחַר נְדָרִים לְבַקֵּר:

26 A wise king winnows out the wicked, And turns the wheel upon them.

כו מְזָרֶה רְשָׁעִים מֶלֶךְ חָכָם וַיָּשֶׁב עֲלֵיהֶם אוֹפָן:

27 The lifebreath of man is the lamp of *Hashem* Revealing all his inmost parts.

כז נֵר יְהוָה נִשְׁמַת אָדָם חֹפֵשׂ כָּל־חַדְרֵי־בָטֶן:

20:22 Put your hope in *Hashem* and He will deliver you Sometimes we see wrongdoing in this world, and it bothers us. This verse teaches that it is not up to man to avenge evil, rather, this is *Hashem*'s duty. However, the fourteenth-century sage Rabbi Levi ben Gershon, better known as *Ralbag*, points out that we should not wish for God's vengeance against our enemies, but only for salvation from their harm. Similarly, the Talmud (*Berachot* 10a) comments, regarding the verse in *Sefer Tehillim* (104:35), that we should not pray for our enemies' demise, but for them to repent of their evil ways.

A sparrow sitting near notes to God left in cracks in the Western Wall

35

28 Faithfulness and loyalty protect the king; He maintains his throne by faithfulness.

כח חֶסֶד וֶאֱמֶת יִצְּרוּ־מֶלֶךְ וְסָעַד בַּחֶסֶד כִּסְאוֹ:

29 The glory of youths is their strength; The majesty of old men is their gray hair.

כט תִּפְאֶרֶת בַּחוּרִים כֹּחָם וַהֲדַר זְקֵנִים שֵׂיבָה:

30 Bruises and wounds are repayment for evil, Striking at one's inmost parts.

ל חַבֻּרוֹת פֶּצַע תַּמְרִיק [תַּמְרוּק] בְּרָע וּמַכּוֹת חַדְרֵי־בָטֶן:

21 1 Like channeled water is the mind of the king in *Hashem*'s hand; He directs it to whatever He wishes.

כא א פַּלְגֵי־מַיִם לֶב־מֶלֶךְ בְּיַד־יְהוָה עַל־כָּל־אֲשֶׁר יַחְפֹּץ יַטֶּנּוּ:

2 All the ways of a man seem right to him, But *Hashem* probes the mind.

ב כָּל־דֶּרֶךְ־אִישׁ יָשָׁר בְּעֵינָיו וְתֹכֵן לִבּוֹת יְהוָה:

3 To do what is right and just Is more desired by *Hashem* than sacrifice.

ג עֲשֹׂה צְדָקָה וּמִשְׁפָּט נִבְחָר לַיהוָה מִזָּבַח:

4 Haughty looks, a proud heart – The tillage of the wicked is sinful.

ד רוּם־עֵינַיִם וּרְחַב־לֵב נִר רְשָׁעִים חַטָּאת:

5 The plans of the diligent make only for gain; All rash haste makes only for loss.

ה מַחְשְׁבוֹת חָרוּץ אַךְ־לְמוֹתָר וְכָל־אָץ אַךְ־לְמַחְסוֹר:

6 Treasures acquired by a lying tongue Are like driven vapor, heading for extinction.

ו פֹּעַל אוֹצָרוֹת בִּלְשׁוֹן שָׁקֶר הֶבֶל נִדָּף מְבַקְשֵׁי־מָוֶת:

7 The violence of the wicked sweeps them away, For they refuse to act justly.

ז שֹׁד־רְשָׁעִים יְגוֹרֵם כִּי מֵאֲנוּ לַעֲשׂוֹת מִשְׁפָּט:

8 The way of a man may be tortuous and strange, Though his actions are blameless and proper.

ח הֲפַכְפַּךְ דֶּרֶךְ אִישׁ וָזָר וְזַךְ יָשָׁר פָּעֳלוֹ:

9 Dwelling in the corner of a roof is better Than a contentious wife in a spacious house.

ט טוֹב לָשֶׁבֶת עַל־פִּנַּת־גָּג מֵאֵשֶׁת מִדְיָנִים וּבֵית חָבֶר:

10 The desire of the wicked is set upon evil; His fellowman finds no favor in his eyes.

י נֶפֶשׁ רָשָׁע אִוְּתָה־רָע לֹא־יֻחַן בְּעֵינָיו רֵעֵהוּ:

11 When a scoffer is punished, the simple man is edified; When a wise man is taught, he gains insight.

יא בַּעֲנָשׁ־לֵץ יֶחְכַּם־פֶּתִי וּבְהַשְׂכִּיל לְחָכָם יִקַּח־דָּעַת:

12 The Righteous One observes the house of the wicked man; He subverts the wicked to their ruin.

יב מַשְׂכִּיל צַדִּיק לְבֵית רָשָׁע מְסַלֵּף רְשָׁעִים לָרָע:

13 Who stops his ears at the cry of the wretched, He too will call and not be answered.

יג אֹטֵם אָזְנוֹ מִזַּעֲקַת־דָּל גַּם־הוּא יִקְרָא וְלֹא יֵעָנֶה:

14 A gift in secret subdues anger, A present in private, fierce rage.

יד מַתָּן בַּסֵּתֶר יִכְפֶּה־אָף וְשֹׁחַד בַּחֵק חֵמָה עַזָּה:

15 Justice done is a joy to the righteous, To evildoers, ruination.

טו שִׂמְחָה לַצַּדִּיק עֲשׂוֹת מִשְׁפָּט וּמְחִתָּה לְפֹעֲלֵי אָוֶן:

16 A man who strays from the path of prudence Will rest in the company of ghosts.

טז אָדָם תּוֹעֶה מִדֶּרֶךְ הַשְׂכֵּל בִּקְהַל רְפָאִים יָנוּחַ:

Proverbs

17 He who loves pleasure comes to want; He who loves wine and oil does not grow rich.

יז אִישׁ מַחְסוֹר אֹהֵב שִׂמְחָה אֹהֵב יַיִן־
וָשֶׁמֶן לֹא יַעֲשִׁיר:

18 The wicked are the ransom of the righteous; The traitor comes in place of the upright.

יח כֹּפֶר לַצַּדִּיק רָשָׁע וְתַחַת יְשָׁרִים בּוֹגֵד:

19 It is better to live in the desert Than with a contentious, vexatious wife.

יט טוֹב שֶׁבֶת בְּאֶרֶץ־מִדְבָּר מֵאֵשֶׁת מדונים
[מִדְיָנִים] וָכָעַס:

20 Precious treasure and oil are in the house of the wise man, And a fool of a man will run through them.

כ אוֹצָר נֶחְמָד וָשֶׁמֶן בִּנְוֵה חָכָם וּכְסִיל
אָדָם יְבַלְּעֶנּוּ:

21 He who strives to do good and kind deeds Attains life, success, and honor.

כא רֹדֵף צְדָקָה וָחָסֶד יִמְצָא חַיִּים צְדָקָה
וְכָבוֹד:

22 One wise man prevailed over a city of warriors And brought down its mighty stronghold.

כב עִיר גִּבֹּרִים עָלָה חָכָם וַיֹּרֶד עֹז מִבְטֶחָה:

23 He who guards his mouth and tongue Guards himself from trouble.

כג שֹׁמֵר פִּיו וּלְשׁוֹנוֹ שֹׁמֵר מִצָּרוֹת נַפְשׁוֹ:

24 The proud, insolent man, scoffer is his name, Acts in a frenzy of insolence.

כד זֵד יָהִיר לֵץ שְׁמוֹ עוֹשֶׂה בְּעֶבְרַת זָדוֹן:

25 The craving of a lazy man kills him, For his hands refuse to work.

כה תַּאֲוַת עָצֵל תְּמִיתֶנּוּ כִּי־מֵאֲנוּ יָדָיו
לַעֲשׂוֹת:

26 All day long he is seized with craving While the righteous man gives without stint.

כו כָּל־הַיּוֹם הִתְאַוָּה תַאֲוָה וְצַדִּיק יִתֵּן וְלֹא
יַחְשֹׂךְ:

27 The sacrifice of the wicked man is an abomination, The more so as he offers it in depravity.

כז זֶבַח רְשָׁעִים תּוֹעֵבָה אַף כִּי־בְזִמָּה
יְבִיאֶנּוּ:

28 A false witness is doomed, But one who really heard will testify with success.

כח עֵד־כְּזָבִים יֹאבֵד וְאִישׁ שׁוֹמֵעַ לָנֶצַח
יְדַבֵּר:

29 The wicked man is brazen-faced; The upright man discerns his course.

כט הֵעֵז אִישׁ רָשָׁע בְּפָנָיו וְיָשָׁר הוּא יכין
[יָבִין] דרכיו [דַּרְכּוֹ]:

30 No wisdom, no prudence, and no counsel Can prevail against *Hashem*.

ל אֵין חָכְמָה וְאֵין תְּבוּנָה וְאֵין עֵצָה לְנֶגֶד
יְהוָה:

31 The horse is readied for the day of battle, But victory comes from *Hashem*.

לא סוּס מוּכָן לְיוֹם מִלְחָמָה וְלַיהוָה
הַתְּשׁוּעָה:

SUS mu-KHAN l'-YOM mil-kha-MAH v'-la-do-NAI ha-t'-shu-AH

22 1 Repute is preferable to great wealth Grace is better than silver and gold.

כב א נִבְחָר שֵׁם מֵעֹשֶׁר רָב מִכֶּסֶף וּמִזָּהָב חֵן
טוֹב:

Beautiful horses in the Golan Heights

21:31 But victory comes from *Hashem*
Throughout the Bible, horses are mentioned as animals of war. Here, King *Shlomo* is emphasizing an important lesson that is no less true today than it was when he said it centuries ago: Man prepares as much as possible, but ultimately, all victory and success comes only from *Hashem*.

2 Rich man and poor man meet; *Hashem* made them both.

ב עָשִׁיר וָרָשׁ נִפְגָּשׁוּ עֹשֵׂה כֻלָּם יְהֹוָה:

3 The shrewd man saw trouble and took cover; The simple kept going and paid the penalty.

ג עָרוּם רָאָה רָעָה ויסתר [וְנִסְתָּר] וּפְתָיִים עָבְרוּ וְנֶעֱנָשׁוּ:

4 The effect of humility is fear of *Hashem*, Wealth, honor, and life.

ד עֵקֶב עֲנָוָה יִרְאַת יְהֹוָה עֹשֶׁר וְכָבוֹד וְחַיִּים:

5 Thorns and snares are in the path of the crooked; He who values his life will keep far from them.

ה צִנִּים פַּחִים בְּדֶרֶךְ עִקֵּשׁ שׁוֹמֵר נַפְשׁוֹ יִרְחַק מֵהֶם:

6 Train a lad in the way he ought to go; He will not swerve from it even in old age.

ו חֲנֹךְ לַנַּעַר עַל־פִּי דַרְכּוֹ גַּם כִּי־יַזְקִין לֹא־יָסוּר מִמֶּנָּה:

7 The rich rule the poor, And the borrower is a slave to the lender.

ז עָשִׁיר בְּרָשִׁים יִמְשׁוֹל וְעֶבֶד לֹוֶה לְאִישׁ מַלְוֶה:

8 He who sows injustice shall reap misfortune; His rod of wrath shall fail.

ח זוֹרֵעַ עַוְלָה יקצור־[יִקְצָר־] אָוֶן וְשֵׁבֶט עֶבְרָתוֹ יִכְלֶה:

9 The generous man is blessed, For he gives of his bread to the poor.

ט טוֹב־עַיִן הוּא יְבֹרָךְ כִּי־נָתַן מִלַּחְמוֹ לַדָּל:

10 Expel the scoffer and contention departs, Quarrel and contumely cease.

י גָּרֵשׁ לֵץ וְיֵצֵא מָדוֹן וְיִשְׁבֹּת דִּין וְקָלוֹן:

11 A pure-hearted friend, His speech is gracious; He has the king for his companion.

יא אֹהֵב טהור־[טְהָר־] לֵב חֵן שְׂפָתָיו רֵעֵהוּ מֶלֶךְ:

12 The eyes of *Hashem* watch the wise man; He subverts the words of the treacherous.

יב עֵינֵי יְהֹוָה נָצְרוּ דָעַת וַיְסַלֵּף דִּבְרֵי בֹגֵד:

13 The lazy man says, "There's a lion in the street; I shall be killed if I step outside."

יג אָמַר עָצֵל אֲרִי בַחוּץ בְּתוֹךְ רְחֹבוֹת אֵרָצֵחַ:

14 The mouth of a forbidden woman is a deep pit; He who is doomed by *Hashem* falls into it.

יד שׁוּחָה עֲמֻקָּה פִּי זָרוֹת זְעוּם יְהֹוָה יפול־[יִפָּל־] שָׁם:

15 If folly settles in the heart of a lad, The rod of discipline will remove it.

טו אִוֶּלֶת קְשׁוּרָה בְלֶב־נָעַר שֵׁבֶט מוּסָר יַרְחִיקֶנָּה מִמֶּנּוּ:

16 To profit by withholding what is due to the poor Is like making gifts to the rich – pure loss.

טז עֹשֵׁק דָּל לְהַרְבּוֹת לוֹ נֹתֵן לְעָשִׁיר אַךְ־לְמַחְסוֹר:

17 Incline your ear and listen to the words of the sages; Pay attention to my wisdom.

יז הַט אָזְנְךָ וּשְׁמַע דִּבְרֵי חֲכָמִים וְלִבְּךָ תָּשִׁית לְדַעְתִּי:

18 It is good that you store them inside you, And that all of them be constantly on your lips,

יח כִּי־נָעִים כִּי־תִשְׁמְרֵם בְּבִטְנֶךָ יִכֹּנוּ יַחְדָּו עַל־שְׂפָתֶיךָ:

19 That you may put your trust in *Hashem*. I let you know today – yes, you –

יט לִהְיוֹת בַּיהֹוָה מִבְטַחֶךָ הוֹדַעְתִּיךָ הַיּוֹם אַף־אָתָּה:

20 Indeed, I wrote down for you a threefold lore, Wise counsel,

כ הֲלֹא כָתַבְתִּי לְךָ שלשום [שָׁלִישִׁים] בְּמוֹעֵצֹת וָדָעַת:

21 To let you know truly reliable words, That you may give a faithful reply to him who sent you.

כא לְהוֹדִיעֲךָ קֹשְׁטְ אִמְרֵי אֱמֶת לְהָשִׁיב אֲמָרִים אֱמֶת לְשֹׁלְחֶיךָ:

22 Do not rob the wretched because he is wretched; Do not crush the poor man in the gate;

כב אַל־תִּגְזָל־דָּל כִּי דַל־הוּא וְאַל־תְּדַכֵּא עָנִי בַשָּׁעַר:

²³ For *Hashem* will take up their cause And despoil those who despoil them of life.

כג כִּי־יְהֹוָה יָרִיב רִיבָם וְקָבַע אֶת־קֹבְעֵיהֶם נָפֶשׁ:

²⁴ Do not associate with an irascible man, Or go about with one who is hot-tempered,

כד אַל־תִּתְרַע אֶת־בַּעַל אָף וְאֶת־אִישׁ חֵמוֹת לֹא תָבוֹא:

²⁵ Lest you learn his ways And find yourself ensnared.

כה פֶּן־תֶּאֱלַף ארחתו [אֹרְחֹתָיו] וְלָקַחְתָּ מוֹקֵשׁ לְנַפְשֶׁךָ:

²⁶ Do not be one of those who give their hand, Who stand surety for debts,

כו אַל־תְּהִי בְתֹקְעֵי־כָף בַּעֹרְבִים מַשָּׁאוֹת:

²⁷ Lest your bed be taken from under you When you have no money to pay.

כז אִם־אֵין־לְךָ לְשַׁלֵּם לָמָּה יִקַּח מִשְׁכָּבְךָ מִתַּחְתֶּיךָ:

²⁸ Do not remove the ancient boundary stone That your ancestors set up.

כח אַל־תַּסֵּג גְּבוּל עוֹלָם אֲשֶׁר עָשׂוּ אֲבוֹתֶיךָ:

al ta-SAYG g'-VUL o-LAM a-SHER a-SU a-vo-TE-kha

²⁹ See a man skilled at his work – He shall attend upon kings; He shall not attend upon obscure men.

כט חָזִיתָ אִישׁ מָהִיר בִּמְלַאכְתּוֹ לִפְנֵי־מְלָכִים יִתְיַצָּב בַּל־יִתְיַצֵּב לִפְנֵי חֲשֻׁכִּים:

23 ¹ When you sit down to dine with a ruler, Consider well who is before you.

גכ א כִּי־תֵשֵׁב לִלְחוֹם אֶת־מוֹשֵׁל בִּין תָּבִין אֶת־אֲשֶׁר לְפָנֶיךָ:

² Thrust a knife into your gullet If you have a large appetite.

ב וְשַׂמְתָּ שַׂכִּין בְּלֹעֶךָ אִם־בַּעַל נֶפֶשׁ אָתָּה:

³ Do not crave for his dainties, For they are counterfeit food.

ג אַל־תִּתְאָו לְמַטְעַמּוֹתָיו וְהוּא לֶחֶם כְּזָבִים:

⁴ Do not toil to gain wealth; Have the sense to desist.

ד אַל־תִּיגַע לְהַעֲשִׁיר מִבִּינָתְךָ חֲדָל:

⁵ You see it, then it is gone; It grows wings and flies away, Like an eagle, heavenward.

ה התעוף [הֲתָעִיף] עֵינֶיךָ בּוֹ וְאֵינֶנּוּ כִּי עָשֹׂה יַעֲשֶׂה־לּוֹ כְנָפַיִם כְּנֶשֶׁר ועיף [יָעוּף] הַשָּׁמָיִם:

ha-ta-EEF ay-NE-kha BO v'-ay-NE-nu KEE a-SOH ya-a-seh
LO kh'-na-FA-yim k'-NE-sher ya-UF ha-sha-MA-yim

An eagle in flight in the Golan Heights

22:28 Do not remove the ancient boundary stone This verse reinforces the significance of a heritage in the Promised Land. When the Israelites arrived there after leaving Egypt, *Hashem* instructed *Moshe* to divide the land by drawing lots. Each tribe was given a region, and each family was assigned a portion of their tribe's land to be passed down through the generations (Numbers 26:52–56). Israel's family bonds to the land are so great, that when *Tzelofchad* died without sons, his daughters demanded the right to inherit their father's portion (Numbers 27). They were granted the inheritance on condition that they marry within their tribe, so the land not be absorbed into another tribe's portion (Numbers 36:6–7).

23:5 Like an eagle, heavenward The eagle flies higher than other birds. According to the medieval commentator *Rashi*, this is the reason why *Hashem* uses the metaphor of an eagle when describing the Exodus from Egypt: "I bore you on eagles' wings and brought you to Me" (Exodus 19:4). As opposed to other birds who carry their young between their legs to protect them from predators flying above them, an eagle carries its young on its back (see Deuteronomy 32:11). Since the eagle flies higher than other birds,

6 Do not eat of a stingy man's food; Do not crave for his dainties;

ו אַל־תִּלְחַם אֶת־לֶחֶם רַע עָיִן וְאַל־תִּתְאָו [תִּתְאָיו] לְמַטְעַמֹּתָיו:

7 He is like one keeping accounts; "Eat and drink," he says to you, But he does not really mean it.

ז כִּי כְּמוֹ־שָׁעַר בְּנַפְשׁוֹ כֶּן־הוּא אֱכֹל וּשְׁתֵה יֹאמַר לָךְ וְלִבּוֹ בַּל־עִמָּךְ:

8 The morsel you eat you will vomit; You will waste your courteous words.

ח פִּתְּךָ־אָכַלְתָּ תְקִיאֶנָּה וְשִׁחַתָּ דְּבָרֶיךָ הַנְּעִימִים:

9 Do not speak to a dullard, For he will disdain your sensible words.

ט בְּאָזְנֵי כְסִיל אַל־תְּדַבֵּר כִּי־יָבוּז לְשֵׂכֶל מִלֶּיךָ:

10 Do not remove ancient boundary stones; Do not encroach upon the field of orphans,

י אַל־תַּסֵּג גְּבוּל עוֹלָם וּבִשְׂדֵי יְתוֹמִים אַל־תָּבֹא:

11 For they have a mighty Kinsman, And He will surely take up their cause with you.

יא כִּי־גֹאֲלָם חָזָק הוּא־יָרִיב אֶת־רִיבָם אִתָּךְ:

12 Apply your mind to discipline And your ears to wise sayings.

יב הָבִיאָה לַמּוּסָר לִבֶּךָ וְאָזְנֶךָ לְאִמְרֵי־דָעַת:

13 Do not withhold discipline from a child; If you beat him with a rod he will not die.

יג אַל־תִּמְנַע מִנַּעַר מוּסָר כִּי־תַכֶּנּוּ בַשֵּׁבֶט לֹא יָמוּת:

14 Beat him with a rod And you will save him from the grave.

יד אַתָּה בַּשֵּׁבֶט תַּכֶּנּוּ וְנַפְשׁוֹ מִשְּׁאוֹל תַּצִּיל:

15 My son, if your mind gets wisdom, My mind, too, will be gladdened.

טו בְּנִי אִם־חָכַם לִבֶּךָ יִשְׂמַח לִבִּי גַם־אָנִי:

16 I shall rejoice with all my heart When your lips speak right things.

טז וְתַעְלֹזְנָה כִלְיוֹתָי בְּדַבֵּר שְׂפָתֶיךָ מֵישָׁרִים:

17 Do not envy sinners in your heart, But only *Hashem*-fearing men, at all times,

יז אַל־יְקַנֵּא לִבְּךָ בַּחַטָּאִים כִּי אִם־בְּיִרְאַת־יְהוָה כָּל־הַיּוֹם:

18 For then you will have a future, And your hope will never fail.

יח כִּי אִם־יֵשׁ אַחֲרִית וְתִקְוָתְךָ לֹא תִכָּרֵת:

19 Listen, my son, and get wisdom; Lead your mind in a [proper] path.

יט שְׁמַע־אַתָּה בְנִי וַחֲכָם וְאַשֵּׁר בַּדֶּרֶךְ לִבֶּךָ:

20 Do not be of those who guzzle wine, Or glut themselves on meat;

כ אַל־תְּהִי בְסֹבְאֵי־יָיִן בְּזֹלֲלֵי בָשָׂר לָמוֹ:

21 For guzzlers and gluttons will be impoverished, And drowsing will clothe you in tatters.

כא כִּי־סֹבֵא וְזוֹלֵל יִוָּרֵשׁ וּקְרָעִים תַּלְבִּישׁ נוּמָה:

Proverbs

22 Listen to your father who begot you; Do not disdain your mother when she is old.

כב שְׁמַע לְאָבִיךָ זֶה יְלָדֶךָ וְאַל־תָּבוּז כִּי־זָקְנָה אִמֶּךָ׃

23 Buy truth and never sell it, And wisdom, discipline, and understanding.

כג אֱמֶת קְנֵה וְאַל־תִּמְכֹּר חָכְמָה וּמוּסָר וּבִינָה׃

24 The father of a righteous man will exult; He who begets a wise son will rejoice in him.

כד גול [גִּיל] יגול [יָגִיל] אֲבִי צַדִּיק יולד [וְיוֹלֵד] חָכָם וישמח־[יִשְׂמַח־] בּוֹ׃

25 Your father and mother will rejoice; She who bore you will exult.

כה יִשְׂמַח־אָבִיךָ וְאִמֶּךָ וְתָגֵל יוֹלַדְתֶּךָ׃

26 Give your mind to me, my son; Let your eyes watch my ways.

כו תְּנָה־בְנִי לִבְּךָ לִי וְעֵינֶיךָ דְּרָכַי תרצנה [תִּצֹּרְנָה]׃

27 A harlot is a deep pit; A forbidden woman is a narrow well.

כז כִּי־שׁוּחָה עֲמֻקָּה זוֹנָה וּבְאֵר צָרָה נָכְרִיָּה׃

28 She too lies in wait as if for prey, And destroys the unfaithful among men.

כח אַף־הִיא כְּחֶתֶף תֶּאֱרֹב וּבוֹגְדִים בְּאָדָם תּוֹסִף׃

29 Who cries, "Woe!" who, "Alas!"; Who has quarrels, who complaints; Who has wounds without cause; Who has bleary eyes?

כט לְמִי אוֹי לְמִי אֲבוֹי לְמִי מדונים [מִדְיָנִים] לְמִי שִׂיחַ לְמִי פְּצָעִים חִנָּם לְמִי חַכְלִלוּת עֵינָיִם׃

30 Those whom wine keeps till the small hours, Those who gather to drain the cups.

ל לַמְאַחֲרִים עַל־הַיָּיִן לַבָּאִים לַחְקֹר מִמְסָךְ׃

31 Do not ogle that red wine As it lends its color to the cup, As it flows on smoothly;

לא אַל־תֵּרֶא יַיִן כִּי יִתְאַדָּם כִּי־יִתֵּן בכיס [בַּכּוֹס] עֵינוֹ יִתְהַלֵּךְ בְּמֵישָׁרִים׃

32 In the end, it bites like a snake; It spits like a basilisk.

לב אַחֲרִיתוֹ כְּנָחָשׁ יִשָּׁךְ וּכְצִפְעֹנִי יַפְרִשׁ׃

33 Your eyes will see strange sights; Your heart will speak distorted things.

לג עֵינֶיךָ יִרְאוּ זָרוֹת וְלִבְּךָ יְדַבֵּר תַּהְפֻּכוֹת׃

34 You will be like one lying in bed on high seas, Like one lying on top of the rigging.

לד וְהָיִיתָ כְּשֹׁכֵב בְּלֶב־יָם וּכְשֹׁכֵב בְּרֹאשׁ חִבֵּל׃

35 "They struck me, but I felt no hurt; They beat me, but I was unaware; As often as I wake, I go after it again."

לה הִכּוּנִי בַל־חָלִיתִי הֲלָמוּנִי בַּל־יָדָעְתִּי מָתַי אָקִיץ אוֹסִיף אֲבַקְשֶׁנּוּ עוֹד׃

24

1 Do not envy evil men Do not desire to be with them;

א אַל־תְּקַנֵּא בְּאַנְשֵׁי רָעָה וְאַל־תתאו [תִּתְאָו] לִהְיוֹת אִתָּם׃

2 For their hearts talk violence, And their lips speak mischief.

ב כִּי־שֹׁד יֶהְגֶּה לִבָּם וְעָמָל שִׂפְתֵיהֶם תְּדַבֵּרְנָה׃

3 A house is built by wisdom, And is established by understanding;

ג בְּחָכְמָה יִבָּנֶה בָּיִת וּבִתְבוּנָה יִתְכּוֹנָן׃

4 By knowledge are its rooms filled With all precious and beautiful things.

ד וּבְדַעַת חֲדָרִים יִמָּלְאוּ כָּל־הוֹן יָקָר וְנָעִים׃

41

5 A wise man is strength; A knowledgeable man exerts power;

ה גֶּבֶר־חָכָם בַּעֽוֹז וְאִישׁ־דַּעַת מְאַמֶּץ־כֹּחַ:

6 For by stratagems you wage war, And victory comes with much planning.

ו כִּי בְתַחְבֻּלוֹת תַּעֲשֶׂה־לְּךָ מִלְחָמָה וּתְשׁוּעָה בְּרֹב יוֹעֵץ:

7 Wisdom is too lofty for a fool; He does not open his mouth in the gate.

ז רָאמוֹת לֶאֱוִיל חָכְמוֹת בַּשַּׁעַר לֹא יִפְתַּח־פִּיהוּ:

8 He who lays plans to do harm Is called by men a schemer.

ח מְחַשֵּׁב לְהָרֵעַ לוֹ בַּעַל־מְזִמּוֹת יִקְרָאוּ:

9 The schemes of folly are sin, And a scoffer is an abomination to men.

ט זִמַּת אִוֶּלֶת חַטָּאת וְתוֹעֲבַת לְאָדָם לֵץ:

10 If you showed yourself slack in time of trouble, Wanting in power,

י הִתְרַפִּיתָ בְּיוֹם צָרָה צַר כֹּחֶכָה:

11 If you refrained from rescuing those taken off to death, Those condemned to slaughter –

יא הַצֵּל לְקֻחִים לַמָּוֶת וּמָטִים לַהֶרֶג אִם־תַּחְשׂוֹךְ:

12 If you say, "We knew nothing of it," Surely He who fathoms hearts will discern [the truth], He who watches over your life will know it, And He will pay each man as he deserves.

יב כִּי־תֹאמַר הֵן לֹא־יָדַעְנוּ זֶה הֲלֹא־תֹכֵן לִבּוֹת הוּא־יָבִין וְנֹצֵר נַפְשְׁךָ הוּא יֵדָע וְהֵשִׁיב לְאָדָם כְּפָעֳלוֹ:

13 My son, eat honey, for it is good; Let its sweet drops be on your palate.

יג אֱכָל־בְּנִי דְבַשׁ כִּי־טוֹב וְנֹפֶת מָתוֹק עַל־חִכֶּךָ:

14 Know: such is wisdom for your soul; If you attain it, there is a future; Your hope will not be cut off.

יד כֵּן דְּעֵה חָכְמָה לְנַפְשֶׁךָ אִם־מָצָאתָ וְיֵשׁ אַחֲרִית וְתִקְוָתְךָ לֹא תִכָּרֵת:

15 Wicked man! Do not lurk by the home of the righteous man; Do no violence to his dwelling.

טו אַל־תֶּאֱרֹב רָשָׁע לִנְוֵה צַדִּיק אַל־תְּשַׁדֵּד רִבְצוֹ:

16 Seven times the righteous man falls and gets up, While the wicked are tripped by one misfortune.

טז כִּי שֶׁבַע יִפּוֹל צַדִּיק וָקָם וּרְשָׁעִים יִכָּשְׁלוּ בְרָעָה:

17 If your enemy falls, do not exult; If he trips, let your heart not rejoice,

יז בִּנְפֹל אֽוֹיִבְךָ [אוֹיִבְךָ] אַל־תִּשְׂמָח וּבִכָּשְׁלוֹ אַל־יָגֵל לִבֶּךָ:

bin-FOL o-yiv-KHA al tis-MAKH u-vi-ka-sh'-LO al ya-GAYL li-BE-kha

18 Lest *Hashem* see it and be displeased, And avert His wrath from him.

יח פֶּן־יִרְאֶה יְהוָה וְרַע בְּעֵינָיו וְהֵשִׁיב מֵעָלָיו אַפּוֹ:

19 Do not be vexed by evildoers; Do not be incensed by the wicked;

יט אַל־תִּתְחַר בַּמְּרֵעִים אַל־תְּקַנֵּא בָּרְשָׁעִים:

24:17 If your enemy falls, do not exult Sadly, it is not uncommon for Israel's enemies to celebrate news of terror attacks by handing out candy in the streets. Here, the Bible emphasizes universal feelings of sympathy and compassion for all, and warns against rejoicing at the downfall of our enemies. For this reason, when the Jewish people celebrate the Exodus at the *Pesach seder* each year, they remove some of the wine in their cups, to sympathize with the Egyptian suffering that happened in the process. In this way, even thousands of years later, the Jewish People symbolically diminish their joy because of the pain experienced by their Egyptian enemies.

Jewish family celebrating the Passover seder

²⁰ For there is no future for the evil man; The lamp of the wicked goes out.

כ כִּי לֹא־תִהְיֶה אַחֲרִית לָרָע נֵר רְשָׁעִים יִדְעָךְ:

²¹ Fear *Hashem*, my son, and the king, And do not mix with dissenters,

כא יְרָא־אֶת־יְהֹוָה בְּנִי וָמֶלֶךְ עִם־שׁוֹנִים אַל־תִּתְעָרֶב:

²² For disaster comes from them suddenly; The doom both decree who can foreknow?

כב כִּי־פִתְאֹם יָקוּם אֵידָם וּפִיד שְׁנֵיהֶם מִי יוֹדֵעַ:

²³ These also are by the sages: It is not right to be partial in judgment.

כג גַּם־אֵלֶּה לַחֲכָמִים הַכֵּר־פָּנִים בְּמִשְׁפָּט בַּל־טוֹב:

²⁴ He who says to the guilty, "You are innocent," Shall be cursed by peoples, Damned by nations;

כד אֹמֵר לְרָשָׁע צַדִּיק אָתָּה יִקְּבֻהוּ עַמִּים יִזְעָמוּהוּ לְאֻמִּים:

²⁵ But it shall go well with them who decide justly; Blessings of good things will light upon them.

כה וְלַמּוֹכִיחִים יִנְעָם וַעֲלֵיהֶם תָּבוֹא בִרְכַּת־טוֹב:

²⁶ Giving a straightforward reply Is like giving a kiss.

כו שְׂפָתַיִם יִשָּׁק מֵשִׁיב דְּבָרִים נְכֹחִים:

²⁷ Put your external affairs in order, Get ready what you have in the field, Then build yourself a home.

כז הָכֵן בַּחוּץ מְלַאכְתֶּךָ וְעַתְּדָהּ בַּשָּׂדֶה לָךְ אַחַר וּבָנִיתָ בֵיתֶךָ:

²⁸ Do not be a witness against your fellow without good cause; Would you mislead with your speech?

כח אַל־תְּהִי עֵד־חִנָּם בְּרֵעֶךָ וַהֲפִתִּיתָ בִּשְׂפָתֶיךָ:

²⁹ Do not say, "I will do to him what he did to me; I will pay the man what he deserves."

כט אַל־תֹּאמַר כַּאֲשֶׁר עָשָׂה־לִי כֵּן אֶעֱשֶׂה־לּוֹ אָשִׁיב לָאִישׁ כְּפָעֳלוֹ:

³⁰ I passed by the field of a lazy man, By the vineyard of a man lacking sense.

ל עַל־שְׂדֵה אִישׁ־עָצֵל עָבַרְתִּי וְעַל־כֶּרֶם אָדָם חֲסַר־לֵב:

³¹ It was all overgrown with thorns; Its surface was covered with chickweed, And its stone fence lay in ruins.

לא וְהִנֵּה עָלָה כֻלּוֹ קִמְּשֹׂנִים כָּסּוּ פָנָיו חֲרֻלִּים וְגֶדֶר אֲבָנָיו נֶהֱרָסָה:

³² I observed and took it to heart; I saw it and learned a lesson.

לב וָאֶחֱזֶה אָנֹכִי אָשִׁית לִבִּי רָאִיתִי לָקַחְתִּי מוּסָר:

³³ A bit more sleep, a bit more slumber, A bit more hugging yourself in bed,

לג מְעַט שֵׁנוֹת מְעַט תְּנוּמוֹת מְעַט חִבֻּק יָדַיִם לִשְׁכָּב:

³⁴ And poverty will come calling upon you, And want, like a man with a shield.

לד וּבָא־מִתְהַלֵּךְ רֵישֶׁךָ וּמַחְסֹרֶיךָ כְּאִישׁ מָגֵן:

25

¹ These too are proverbs of *Shlomo*, which the men of King *Chizkiyahu* of *Yehuda* copied:

ה א גַּם־אֵלֶּה מִשְׁלֵי שְׁלֹמֹה אֲשֶׁר הֶעְתִּיקוּ אַנְשֵׁי חִזְקִיָּה מֶלֶךְ־יְהוּדָה:

² It is the glory of *Hashem* to conceal a matter, And the glory of a king to plumb a matter.

ב כְּבֹד אֱלֹהִים הַסְתֵּר דָּבָר וּכְבֹד מְלָכִים חֲקֹר דָּבָר:

k'-VOD e-lo-HEEM has-TAYR da-VAR ukh-VOD m'-la-KHEEM kha-KOR da-VAR

A menorah lit in commemoration of the miracle of Chanukkah

25:2 It is the glory of *Hashem* to conceal a matter The glory of earthly kings is made greater through scrutiny and investigation, both on their own part and when conducted by others. When the kings search out the truth in order to do justice, they bring honor to themselves, and when oth-

3 Like the heavens in their height, like the earth in its depth, Is the mind of kings – unfathomable.

ג שָׁמַיִם לָרוּם וָאָרֶץ לָעֹמֶק וְלֵב מְלָכִים אֵין חֵקֶר:

4 The dross having been separated from the silver, A vessel emerged for the smith.

ד הָגוֹ סִיגִים מִכָּסֶף וַיֵּצֵא לַצֹּרֵף כֶּלִי:

5 Remove the wicked from the king's presence, And his throne will be established in justice.

ה הָגוֹ רָשָׁע לִפְנֵי־מֶלֶךְ וְיִכּוֹן בַּצֶּדֶק כִּסְאוֹ:

6 Do not exalt yourself in the king's presence; Do not stand in the place of nobles.

ו אַל־תִּתְהַדַּר לִפְנֵי־מֶלֶךְ וּבִמְקוֹם גְּדֹלִים אַל־תַּעֲמֹד:

7 For it is better to be told, "Step up here," Than to be degraded in the presence of the great. Do not let what your eyes have seen

ז כִּי טוֹב אֲמָר־לְךָ עֲלֵה הֵנָּה מֵהַשְׁפִּילְךָ לִפְנֵי נָדִיב אֲשֶׁר רָאוּ עֵינֶיךָ:

8 Be vented rashly in a quarrel; Think of what it will effect in the end, When your fellow puts you to shame.

ח אַל־תֵּצֵא לָרִב מַהֵר פֶּן מַה־תַּעֲשֶׂה בְּאַחֲרִיתָהּ בְּהַכְלִים אֹתְךָ רֵעֶךָ:

9 Defend your right against your fellow, But do not give away the secrets of another,

ט רִיבְךָ רִיב אֶת־רֵעֶךָ וְסוֹד אַחֵר אַל־תְּגָל:

10 Lest he who hears it reproach you, And your bad repute never end.

י פֶּן־יְחַסֶּדְךָ שֹׁמֵעַ וְדִבָּתְךָ לֹא תָשׁוּב:

11 Like golden apples in silver showpieces Is a phrase well turned.

יא תַּפּוּחֵי זָהָב בְּמַשְׂכִּיּוֹת כָּסֶף דָּבָר דָּבֻר עַל־אָפְנָיו:

12 Like a ring of gold, a golden ornament, Is a wise man's reproof in a receptive ear.

יב נֶזֶם זָהָב וַחֲלִי־כָתֶם מוֹכִיחַ חָכָם עַל־אֹזֶן שֹׁמָעַת:

13 Like the coldness of snow at harvesttime Is a trusty messenger to those who send him; He lifts his master's spirits.

יג כְּצִנַּת־שֶׁלֶג בְּיוֹם קָצִיר צִיר נֶאֱמָן לְשֹׁלְחָיו וְנֶפֶשׁ אֲדֹנָיו יָשִׁיב:

14 Like clouds, wind – but no rain – Is one who boasts of gifts not given.

יד נְשִׂיאִים וְרוּחַ וְגֶשֶׁם אָיִן אִישׁ מִתְהַלֵּל בְּמַתַּת־שָׁקֶר:

15 Through forbearance a ruler may be won over; A gentle tongue can break bones.

טו בְּאֹרֶךְ אַפַּיִם יְפֻתֶּה קָצִין וְלָשׁוֹן רַכָּה תִּשְׁבָּר־גָּרֶם:

16 If you find honey, eat only what you need, Lest, surfeiting yourself, you throw it up.

טז דְּבַשׁ מָצָאתָ אֱכֹל דַּיֶּךָ פֶּן־תִּשְׂבָּעֶנּוּ וַהֲקֵאתוֹ:

17 Visit your neighbor sparingly, Lest he have his surfeit of you and loathe you.

יז הֹקַר רַגְלְךָ מִבֵּית רֵעֶךָ פֶּן־יִשְׂבָּעֲךָ וּשְׂנֵאֶךָ:

Proverbs

ers look into their actions, they respect such leaders for their righteousness. *Hashem*'s glory, on the other hand, is made greater by concealment. His miracles and actions are beyond human understanding, and though they are recorded in the Bible, many are shrouded in mystery.

18 Like a club, a sword, a sharpened arrow, Is a man who testifies falsely against his fellow.

יח מֵפִיץ וְחֶרֶב וְחֵץ שָׁנוּן אִישׁ עֹנֶה בְרֵעֵהוּ עֵד שָׁקֶר:

19 Like a loose tooth and an unsteady leg, Is a treacherous support in time of trouble.

יט שֵׁן רֹעָה וְרֶגֶל מוּעָדֶת מִבְטָח בּוֹגֵד בְּיוֹם צָרָה:

20 Disrobing on a chilly day, Like vinegar on natron, Is one who sings songs to a sorrowful soul.

כ מַעֲדֶה בֶּגֶד בְּיוֹם קָרָה חֹמֶץ עַל־נָתֶר וְשָׁר בַּשִּׁרִים עַל לֶב־רָע:

21 If your enemy is hungry, give him bread to eat; If he is thirsty, give him water to drink.

כא אִם־רָעֵב שֹׂנַאֲךָ הַאֲכִלֵהוּ לָחֶם וְאִם־ צָמֵא הַשְׁקֵהוּ מָיִם:

22 You will be heaping live coals on his head, And *Hashem* will reward you.

כב כִּי גֶחָלִים אַתָּה חֹתֶה עַל־רֹאשׁוֹ וַיהֹוָה יְשַׁלֶּם־לָךְ:

23 A north wind produces rain, And whispered words, a glowering face.

כג רוּחַ צָפוֹן תְּחוֹלֵל גָּשֶׁם וּפָנִים נִזְעָמִים לְשׁוֹן סָתֶר:

24 Dwelling in the corner of a roof is better Than a contentious woman in a spacious house.

כד טוֹב שֶׁבֶת עַל־פִּנַּת־גָּג מֵאֵשֶׁת מדונים [מִדְיָנִים] וּבֵית חָבֶר:

25 Like cold water to a parched throat Is good news from a distant land.

כה מַיִם קָרִים עַל־נֶפֶשׁ עֲיֵפָה וּשְׁמוּעָה טוֹבָה מֵאֶרֶץ מֶרְחָק:

26 Like a muddied spring, a ruined fountain, Is a righteous man fallen before a wicked one.

כו מַעְיָן נִרְפָּשׂ וּמָקוֹר מָשְׁחָת צַדִּיק מָט לִפְנֵי־רָשָׁע:

27 It is not good to eat much honey, Nor is it honorable to search for honor.

כז אָכֹל דְּבַשׁ הַרְבּוֹת לֹא־טוֹב וְחֵקֶר כְּבֹדָם כָּבוֹד:

28 Like an open city without walls Is a man whose temper is uncurbed.

כח עִיר פְּרוּצָה אֵין חוֹמָה אִישׁ אֲשֶׁר אֵין מַעְצָר לְרוּחוֹ:

26 1 Like snow in summer and rain at harvest-time, So honor is not fitting for a dullard.

כו א כַּשֶּׁלֶג בַּקַּיִץ וְכַמָּטָר בַּקָּצִיר כֵּן לֹא־ נָאוֶה לִכְסִיל כָּבוֹד:

2 As a sparrow must flit and a swallow fly, So a gratuitous curse must backfire.

ב כַּצִּפּוֹר לָנוּד כַּדְּרוֹר לָעוּף כֵּן קִלְלַת חִנָּם לא [לוֹ] תָבֹא:

3 A whip for a horse and a bridle for a donkey, And a rod for the back of dullards.

ג שׁוֹט לַסּוּס מֶתֶג לַחֲמוֹר וְשֵׁבֶט לְגֵו כְּסִילִים:

4 Do not answer a dullard in accord with his folly, Else you will become like him.

ד אַל־תַּעַן כְּסִיל כְּאִוַּלְתּוֹ פֶּן־תִּשְׁוֶה־לּוֹ גַם־אָתָּה:

5 Answer a dullard in accord with his folly, Else he will think himself wise.

ה עֲנֵה כְסִיל כְּאִוַּלְתּוֹ פֶּן־יִהְיֶה חָכָם בְּעֵינָיו:

6 He who sends a message by a dullard Will wear out legs and must put up with lawlessness.

ו מְקַצֶּה רַגְלַיִם חָמָס שֹׁתֶה שֹׁלֵחַ דְּבָרִים בְּיַד־כְּסִיל:

7 As legs hang limp on a cripple, So is a proverb in the mouth of dullards.

ז דַּלְיוּ שֹׁקַיִם מִפִּסֵּחַ וּמָשָׁל בְּפִי כְסִילִים:

8 Like a pebble in a sling, So is paying honor to a dullard.

ח כִּצְרוֹר אֶבֶן בְּמַרְגֵּמָה כֵּן־נוֹתֵן לִכְסִיל כָּבוֹד:

9 As a thorn comes to the hand of a drunkard, So a proverb to the mouth of a dullard.

חוֹחַ עָלָה בְיַד־שָׁכּוֹר וּמָשָׁל בְּפִי כְסִילִים: ט

10 A master can produce anything, But he who hires a dullard is as one who hires transients.

רַב מְחוֹלֵל־כֹּל וְשֹׂכֵר כְּסִיל וְשֹׂכֵר עֹבְרִים: י

11 As a dog returns to his vomit, So a dullard repeats his folly.

כְּכֶלֶב שָׁב עַל־קֵאוֹ כְּסִיל שׁוֹנֶה בְאִוַּלְתּוֹ: יא

12 If you see a man who thinks himself wise, There is more hope for a dullard than for him.

רָאִיתָ אִישׁ חָכָם בְּעֵינָיו תִּקְוָה לִכְסִיל מִמֶּנּוּ: יב

13 A lazy man says, "There's a cub on the road, a lion in the squares."

אָמַר עָצֵל שַׁחַל בַּדָּרֶךְ אֲרִי בֵּין הָרְחֹבוֹת: יג

14 The door turns on its hinge, And the lazy man on his bed.

הַדֶּלֶת תִּסּוֹב עַל־צִירָהּ וְעָצֵל עַל־מִטָּתוֹ: יד

15 The lazy man buries his hand in the bowl; He will not even bring it to his mouth.

טָמַן עָצֵל יָדוֹ בַּצַּלָּחַת נִלְאָה לַהֲשִׁיבָהּ אֶל־פִּיו: טו

16 The lazy man thinks himself wiser Than seven men who give good advice.

חָכָם עָצֵל בְּעֵינָיו מִשִּׁבְעָה מְשִׁיבֵי טָעַם: טז

17 A passerby who gets embroiled in someone else's quarrel Is like one who seizes a dog by its ears.

מַחֲזִיק בְּאָזְנֵי־כָלֶב עֹבֵר מִתְעַבֵּר עַל־רִיב לֹּא־לוֹ: יז

18 Like a madman scattering deadly firebrands, arrows,

כְּמִתְלַהְלֵהַּ הַיֹּרֶה זִקִּים חִצִּים וָמָוֶת: יח

19 Is one who cheats his fellow and says, "I was only joking."

כֵּן־אִישׁ רִמָּה אֶת־רֵעֵהוּ וְאָמַר הֲלֹא־מְשַׂחֵק אָנִי: יט

20 For lack of wood a fire goes out, And without a querulous man contention is stilled.

בְּאֶפֶס עֵצִים תִּכְבֶּה־אֵשׁ וּבְאֵין נִרְגָּן יִשְׁתֹּק מָדוֹן: כ

b'-E-fes ay-TZEEM tikh-beh AYSH uv-AYN nir-GAN yish-TOK ma-DON

21 Charcoal for embers and wood for a fire And a contentious man for kindling strife.

פֶּחָם לְגֶחָלִים וְעֵצִים לְאֵשׁ וְאִישׁ מדונים [מִדְיָנִים] לְחַרְחַר־רִיב: כא

22 The words of a querulous man are bruising; They penetrate one's inmost parts.

דִּבְרֵי נִרְגָּן כְּמִתְלַהֲמִים וְהֵם יָרְדוּ חַדְרֵי־בָטֶן: כב

Israeli youth celebrate the minor Jewish holiday of Lag Ba'Omer with a bonfire

26:20 And without a querulous man contention is stilled Rumors and slander add fuel to the fire of human contention. Just as a fire will burn itself out when it runs out of wood, so too, a disagreement will end naturally if the parties involved are not continually provoked by gossip. The *Torah* warns against speaking ill about others. The verse in *Sefer Vayikra* (19:16), "Do not deal basely with your countrymen," is usually translated as "thou shalt not go up and down as a tale-bearer among thy people." Speech is so powerful and potentially dangerous that, according to the Sages (*Erchin* 15a), the tongue had to be hidden behind two protective barriers, the lips and the teeth, in order to protect it from being used for slander. Indeed, it was the slander of the spies, who spoke evil about the Land of Israel, which delayed entry into the Holy Land and caused the Nation of Israel to wander in the desert for forty years.

23 Base silver laid over earthenware Are ardent lips with an evil mind.

כג כֶּסֶף סִיגִים מְצֻפֶּה עַל־חָרֶשׂ שְׂפָתַיִם
דֹּלְקִים וְלֶב־רָע:

24 An enemy dissembles with his speech, Inwardly he harbors deceit.

כד בשפתו [בִּשְׂפָתָיו] יִנָּכֵר שׂוֹנֵא וּבְקִרְבּוֹ
יָשִׁית מִרְמָה:

25 Though he be fair-spoken do not trust him, For seven abominations are in his mind.

כה כִּי־יְחַנֵּן קוֹלוֹ אַל־תַּאֲמֶן־בּוֹ כִּי שֶׁבַע
תּוֹעֵבוֹת בְּלִבּוֹ:

26 His hatred may be concealed by dissimulation, But his evil will be exposed to public view.

כו תִּכַּסֶּה שִׂנְאָה בְּמַשָּׁאוֹן תִּגָּלֶה רָעָתוֹ
בְקָהָל:

27 He who digs a pit will fall in it, And whoever rolls a stone, it will roll back on him.

כז כֹּרֶה־שַּׁחַת בָּהּ יִפֹּל וְגֹלֵל אֶבֶן אֵלָיו
תָּשׁוּב:

28 A lying tongue hates those crushed by it; Smooth speech throws one down.

כח לְשׁוֹן־שֶׁקֶר יִשְׂנָא דַכָּיו וּפֶה חָלָק יַעֲשֶׂה
מִדְחֶה:

27 1 Do not boast of tomorrow For you do not know what the day will bring.

א אַל־תִּתְהַלֵּל בְּיוֹם מָחָר כִּי לֹא־תֵדַע
מַה־יֵּלֶד יוֹם:

2 Let the mouth of another praise you, not yours, The lips of a stranger, not your own.

ב יְהַלֶּלְךָ זָר וְלֹא־פִיךָ נָכְרִי וְאַל־שְׂפָתֶיךָ:

3 A stone has weight, sand is heavy, But a fool's vexation outweighs them both.

ג כֹּבֶד־אֶבֶן וְנֵטֶל הַחוֹל וְכַעַס אֱוִיל כָּבֵד
מִשְּׁנֵיהֶם:

4 There is the cruelty of fury, the overflowing of anger, But who can withstand jealousy?

ד אַכְזְרִיּוּת חֵמָה וְשֶׁטֶף אָף וּמִי יַעֲמֹד
לִפְנֵי קִנְאָה:

5 Open reproof is better than concealed love.

ה טוֹבָה תּוֹכַחַת מְגֻלָּה מֵאַהֲבָה מְסֻתָּרֶת:

6 Wounds by a loved one are long lasting; The kisses of an enemy are profuse.

ו נֶאֱמָנִים פִּצְעֵי אוֹהֵב וְנַעְתָּרוֹת נְשִׁיקוֹת
שׂוֹנֵא:

ne-e-ma-NEEM pitz-AY o-HAYV v'-na-ta-ROT n'-shee-KOT so-NAY

7 A sated person disdains honey, But to a hungry man anything bitter seems sweet.

ז נֶפֶשׁ שְׂבֵעָה תָּבוּס נֹפֶת וְנֶפֶשׁ רְעֵבָה
כָּל־מַר מָתוֹק:

8 Like a sparrow wandering from its nest Is a man who wanders from his home.

ח כְּצִפּוֹר נוֹדֶדֶת מִן־קִנָּהּ כֵּן־אִישׁ נוֹדֵד
מִמְּקוֹמוֹ:

9 Oil and incense gladden the heart, And the sweetness of a friend is better than one's own counsel.

ט שֶׁמֶן וּקְטֹרֶת יְשַׂמַּח־לֵב וּמֶתֶק רֵעֵהוּ
מֵעֲצַת־נָפֶשׁ:

27:6 The kisses of an enemy are profuse With a trusted friend, even actions that seem hurtful ultimately turn out to be beneficial. A well-timed reprimand from someone who loves you can guide you to a better course of action. An enemy, however, should not be trusted. Even if he appears to offer love and support, he will ultimately lead you astray. This idea is reflected in the words of the prophets who rebuke the Israelites for putting their trust in other nations, such as Assyria and Egypt, instead of *Hashem*. Ultimately, they were let down by their enemies who determined they had nothing more to gain from helping the Jewish people (see Hosea 8:8–9).

Children waving the Israeli flag at the beach

¹⁰ Do not desert your friend and your father's friend; Do not enter your brother's house in your time of misfortune; A close neighbor is better than a distant brother.

¹¹ Get wisdom, my son, and gladden my heart, That I may have what to answer those who taunt me.

¹² The shrewd man saw trouble and took cover; The simple kept going and paid the penalty.

¹³ Seize his garment, for he stood surety for another; Take it as a pledge, [for he stood surety] for an unfamiliar woman.

¹⁴ He who greets his fellow loudly early in the morning Shall have it reckoned to him as a curse.

¹⁵ An endless dripping on a rainy day And a contentious wife are alike;

¹⁶ As soon repress her as repress the wind, Or declare one's right hand to be oil.

¹⁷ As iron sharpens iron So a man sharpens the wit of his friend.

¹⁸ He who tends a fig tree will enjoy its fruit, And he who cares for his master will be honored.

¹⁹ As face answers to face in water, So does one man's heart to another.

²⁰ Sheol and Abaddon cannot be satisfied, Nor can the eyes of man be satisfied.

²¹ For silver – the crucible, for gold – the furnace, And a man is tested by his praise.

²² Even if you pound the fool in a mortar With a pestle along with grain, His folly will not leave him.

²³ Mind well the looks of your flock; Pay attention to your herds;

²⁴ For property does not last forever, Or a crown for all generations.

²⁵ Grass vanishes, new grass appears, And the herbage of the hills is gathered in.

²⁶ The lambs will provide you with clothing, The he-goats, the price of a field.

²⁷ The goats' milk will suffice for your food, The food of your household, And the maintenance of your maids.

י רֵעֲךָ וְרֵעֶה [וְרֵעַ] אָבִיךָ אַל־תַּעֲזֹב וּבֵית אָחִיךָ אַל־תָּבוֹא בְּיוֹם אֵידֶךָ טוֹב שָׁכֵן קָרוֹב מֵאָח רָחוֹק:

יא חֲכַם בְּנִי וְשַׂמַּח לִבִּי וְאָשִׁיבָה חֹרְפִי דָבָר:

יב עָרוּם רָאָה רָעָה נִסְתָּר פְּתָאיִם עָבְרוּ נֶעֱנָשׁוּ:

יג קַח־בִּגְדוֹ כִּי־עָרַב זָר וּבְעַד נָכְרִיָּה חַבְלֵהוּ:

יד מְבָרֵךְ רֵעֵהוּ בְּקוֹל גָּדוֹל בַּבֹּקֶר הַשְׁכֵּים קְלָלָה תֵּחָשֶׁב לוֹ:

טו דֶּלֶף טוֹרֵד בְּיוֹם סַגְרִיר וְאֵשֶׁת מדונים [מִדְיָנִים] נִשְׁתָּוָה:

טז צֹפְנֶיהָ צָפַן־רוּחַ וְשֶׁמֶן יְמִינוֹ יִקְרָא:

יז בַּרְזֶל בְּבַרְזֶל יָחַד וְאִישׁ יַחַד פְּנֵי־רֵעֵהוּ:

יח נֹצֵר תְּאֵנָה יֹאכַל פִּרְיָהּ וְשֹׁמֵר אֲדֹנָיו יְכֻבָּד:

יט כַּמַּיִם הַפָּנִים לַפָּנִים כֵּן לֵב־הָאָדָם לָאָדָם:

כ שְׁאוֹל וַאֲבַדה [וַאֲבַדּוֹ] לֹא תִשְׂבַּעְנָה וְעֵינֵי הָאָדָם לֹא תִשְׂבַּעְנָה:

כא מַצְרֵף לַכֶּסֶף וְכוּר לַזָּהָב וְאִישׁ לְפִי מַהֲלָלוֹ:

כב אִם תִּכְתּוֹשׁ־אֶת־הָאֱוִיל בַּמַּכְתֵּשׁ בְּתוֹךְ הָרִיפוֹת בַּעֱלִי לֹא־תָסוּר מֵעָלָיו אִוַּלְתּוֹ:

כג יָדֹעַ תֵּדַע פְּנֵי צֹאנֶךָ שִׁית לִבְּךָ לַעֲדָרִים:

כד כִּי לֹא לְעוֹלָם חֹסֶן וְאִם־נֵזֶר לְדוֹר דּוֹר [וָדוֹר]:

כה גָּלָה חָצִיר וְנִרְאָה־דָשֶׁא וְנֶאֶסְפוּ עִשְּׂבוֹת הָרִים:

כו כְּבָשִׂים לִלְבוּשֶׁךָ וּמְחִיר שָׂדֶה עַתּוּדִים:

כז וְדֵי חֲלֵב עִזִּים לְלַחְמְךָ לְלֶחֶם בֵּיתֶךָ וְחַיִּים לְנַעֲרוֹתֶיךָ:

28 ¹ The wicked flee though no one gives chase, But the righteous are as confident as a lion.

ח א נָסוּ וְאֵין־רֹדֵף רָשָׁע וְצַדִּיקִים כִּכְפִיר יִבְטָח:

² When there is rebellion in the land, many are its rulers; But with a man who has understanding and knowledge, stability will last.

ב בְּפֶשַׁע אֶרֶץ רַבִּים שָׂרֶיהָ וּבְאָדָם מֵבִין יֹדֵעַ כֵּן יַאֲרִיךְ:

³ A poor man who withholds what is due to the wretched Is like a destructive rain that leaves no food.

ג גֶּבֶר רָשׁ וְעֹשֵׁק דַּלִּים מָטָר סֹחֵף וְאֵין לָחֶם:

⁴ Those who forsake instruction praise the wicked, But those who heed instruction fight them.

ד עֹזְבֵי תוֹרָה יְהַלְלוּ רָשָׁע וְשֹׁמְרֵי תוֹרָה יִתְגָּרוּ בָם:

⁵ Evil men cannot discern judgment, But those who seek *Hashem* discern all things.

ה אַנְשֵׁי־רָע לֹא־יָבִינוּ מִשְׁפָּט וּמְבַקְשֵׁי יְהוָה יָבִינוּ כֹל:

⁶ Better is a poor man who lives blamelessly Than a rich man whose ways are crooked.

ו טוֹב־רָשׁ הוֹלֵךְ בְּתֻמּוֹ מֵעִקֵּשׁ דְּרָכַיִם וְהוּא עָשִׁיר:

⁷ An intelligent son heeds instruction, But he who keeps company with gluttons disgraces his father.

ז נוֹצֵר תּוֹרָה בֵּן מֵבִין וְרֹעֶה זוֹלְלִים יַכְלִים אָבִיו:

⁸ He who increases his wealth by loans at discount or interest Amasses it for one who is generous to the poor.

ח מַרְבֶּה הוֹנוֹ בְּנֶשֶׁךְ ובתרבית [וְתַרְבִּית] לְחוֹנֵן דַּלִּים יִקְבְּצֶנּוּ:

mar-BEH ho-NO b'-NE-shekh v'-tar-BEET l'-kho-NAYN da-LEEM yik-b'-TZE-nu

⁹ He who turns a deaf ear to instruction – His prayer is an abomination.

ט מֵסִיר אָזְנוֹ מִשְּׁמֹעַ תּוֹרָה גַּם־תְּפִלָּתוֹ תּוֹעֵבָה:

¹⁰ He who misleads the upright into an evil course Will fall into his own pit, But the blameless will prosper.

י מַשְׁגֶּה יְשָׁרִים בְּדֶרֶךְ רָע בִּשְׁחוּתוֹ הוּא־יִפּוֹל וּתְמִימִים יִנְחֲלוּ־טוֹב:

¹¹ A rich man is clever in his own eyes, But a perceptive poor man can see through him.

יא חָכָם בְּעֵינָיו אִישׁ עָשִׁיר וְדַל מֵבִין יַחְקְרֶנּוּ:

¹² When the righteous exult there is great glory, But when the wicked rise up men make themselves scarce.

יב בַּעֲלֹץ צַדִּיקִים רַבָּה תִפְאָרֶת וּבְקוּם רְשָׁעִים יְחֻפַּשׂ אָדָם:

¹³ He who covers up his faults will not succeed; He who confesses and gives them up will find mercy.

יג מְכַסֶּה פְשָׁעָיו לֹא יַצְלִיחַ וּמוֹדֶה וְעֹזֵב יְרֻחָם:

¹⁴ Happy is the man who is anxious always, But he who hardens his heart falls into misfortune.

יד אַשְׁרֵי אָדָם מְפַחֵד תָּמִיד וּמַקְשֶׁה לִבּוֹ יִפּוֹל בְּרָעָה:

Rabbi Tuly Weisz delivering food packages to Israel's poor

28:8 Amasses it for one who is generous to the poor Despite sayings to the contrary, sometimes it seems that the wicked do prosper. After all, if crime didn't pay, nobody would bother to try. This concerned even the greatest of biblical personalities, such as *Yirmiyahu*, who asks, "Wherefore does the way of the wicked prosper?" (Jeremiah 12:1). However, King *Shlomo* reassures us, one who becomes rich through dishonest means merely accumulates the wealth for the benefit of the righteous, as *Hashem* will ensure it arrives in their possession in the end.

Proverbs

15 A roaring lion and a prowling bear Is a wicked man ruling a helpless people.

טו אֲרִי־נֹהֵם וְדֹב שׁוֹקֵק מֹשֵׁל רָשָׁע עַל עַם־דָּל:

16 A prince who lacks understanding is very oppressive; He who spurns ill-gotten gains will live long.

טז נָגִיד חֲסַר תְּבוּנוֹת וְרַב מַעֲשַׁקּוֹת שֹׂנֵא [שֹׂנֵא] בֶצַע יַאֲרִיךְ יָמִים:

17 A man oppressed by bloodguilt will flee to a pit; Let none give him support.

יז אָדָם עָשֻׁק בְּדַם־נָפֶשׁ עַד־בּוֹר יָנוּס אַל־יִתְמְכוּ־בוֹ:

18 He who lives blamelessly will be delivered, But he who is crooked in his ways will fall all at once.

יח הוֹלֵךְ תָּמִים יִוָּשֵׁעַ וְנֶעְקַשׁ דְּרָכַיִם יִפּוֹל בְּאֶחָת:

19 He who tills his land will have food in plenty, But he who pursues vanities will have poverty in plenty.

יט עֹבֵד אַדְמָתוֹ יִשְׂבַּע־לָחֶם וּמְרַדֵּף רֵקִים יִשְׂבַּע־רִישׁ:

20 A dependable man will receive many blessings, But one in a hurry to get rich will not go unpunished.

כ אִישׁ אֱמוּנוֹת רַב־בְּרָכוֹת וְאָץ לְהַעֲשִׁיר לֹא יִנָּקֶה:

21 To be partial is not right; A man may do wrong for a piece of bread.

כא הַכֵּר־פָּנִים לֹא־טוֹב וְעַל־פַּת־לֶחֶם יִפְשַׁע־גָּבֶר:

22 A miserly man runs after wealth; He does not realize that loss will overtake it.

כב נִבְהָל לַהוֹן אִישׁ רַע עָיִן וְלֹא־יֵדַע כִּי־חֶסֶר יְבֹאֶנּוּ:

23 He who reproves a man will in the end Find more favor than he who flatters him.

כג מוֹכִיחַ אָדָם אַחֲרַי חֵן יִמְצָא מִמַּחֲלִיק לָשׁוֹן:

24 He who robs his father and mother and says, "It is no offense," Is a companion to vandals.

כד גּוֹזֵל אָבִיו וְאִמּוֹ וְאֹמֵר אֵין־פָּשַׁע חָבֵר הוּא לְאִישׁ מַשְׁחִית:

25 A greedy man provokes quarrels, But he who trusts *Hashem* shall enjoy prosperity.

כה רְחַב־נֶפֶשׁ יְגָרֶה מָדוֹן וּבוֹטֵחַ עַל־יְהֹוָה יְדֻשָּׁן:

26 He who trusts his own instinct is a dullard, But he who lives by wisdom shall escape.

כו בּוֹטֵחַ בְּלִבּוֹ הוּא כְסִיל וְהוֹלֵךְ בְּחָכְמָה הוּא יִמָּלֵט:

27 He who gives to the poor will not be in want, But he who shuts his eyes will be roundly cursed.

כז נוֹתֵן לָרָשׁ אֵין מַחְסוֹר וּמַעְלִים עֵינָיו רַב־מְאֵרוֹת:

28 When the wicked rise up, men go into hiding, But when they perish the righteous increase.

כח בְּקוּם רְשָׁעִים יִסָּתֵר אָדָם וּבְאָבְדָם יִרְבּוּ צַדִּיקִים:

29 1 One oft reproved may become stiffnecked, But he will be suddenly broken beyond repair.

כט א אִישׁ תּוֹכָחוֹת מַקְשֶׁה־עֹרֶף פֶּתַע יִשָּׁבֵר וְאֵין מַרְפֵּא:

2 When the righteous become great the people rejoice, But when the wicked dominate the people groan.

ב בִּרְבוֹת צַדִּיקִים יִשְׂמַח הָעָם וּבִמְשֹׁל רָשָׁע יֵאָנַח עָם:

3 A man who loves wisdom brings joy to his father, But he who keeps company with harlots will lose his wealth.

ג אִישׁ־אֹהֵב חָכְמָה יְשַׂמַּח אָבִיו וְרֹעֶה זוֹנוֹת יְאַבֶּד־הוֹן:

4 By justice a king sustains the land, But a fraudulent man tears it down.

ד מֶלֶךְ בְּמִשְׁפָּט יַעֲמִיד אָרֶץ וְאִישׁ תְּרוּמוֹת יֶהֶרְסֶנָּה:

5 A man who flatters his fellow Spreads a net for his feet.

ה גֶּבֶר מַחֲלִיק עַל־רֵעֵהוּ רֶשֶׁת פּוֹרֵשׂ עַל־פְּעָמָיו:

6 An evil man's offenses are a trap for himself, But the righteous sing out joyously.

ו בְּפֶשַׁע אִישׁ רָע מוֹקֵשׁ וְצַדִּיק יָרוּן וְשָׂמֵחַ:

7 A righteous man is concerned with the cause of the wretched; A wicked man cannot understand such concern.

ז יֹדֵעַ צַדִּיק דִּין דַּלִּים רָשָׁע לֹא־יָבִין דָּעַת:

8 Scoffers inflame a city, But the wise allay anger.

ח אַנְשֵׁי לָצוֹן יָפִיחוּ קִרְיָה וַחֲכָמִים יָשִׁיבוּ אָף:

9 When a wise man enters into litigation with a fool There is ranting and ridicule, but no satisfaction.

ט אִישׁ־חָכָם נִשְׁפָּט אֶת־אִישׁ אֱוִיל וְרָגַז וְשָׂחַק וְאֵין נָחַת:

10 Bloodthirsty men detest the blameless, But the upright seek them out.

י אַנְשֵׁי דָמִים יִשְׂנְאוּ־תָם וִישָׁרִים יְבַקְשׁוּ נַפְשׁוֹ:

11 A dullard vents all his rage, But a wise man calms it down.

יא כָּל־רוּחוֹ יוֹצִיא כְסִיל וְחָכָם בְּאָחוֹר יְשַׁבְּחֶנָּה:

12 A ruler who listens to lies, All his ministers will be wicked.

יב מֹשֵׁל מַקְשִׁיב עַל־דְּבַר־שָׁקֶר כָּל־מְשָׁרְתָיו רְשָׁעִים:

13 A poor man and a fraudulent man meet; *Hashem* gives luster to the eyes of both.

יג רָשׁ וְאִישׁ תְּכָכִים נִפְגָּשׁוּ מֵאִיר־עֵינֵי שְׁנֵיהֶם יְהֹוָה:

14 A king who judges the wretched honestly, His throne will be established forever.

יד מֶלֶךְ שׁוֹפֵט בֶּאֱמֶת דַּלִּים כִּסְאוֹ לָעַד יִכּוֹן:

15 Rod and reproof produce wisdom, But a lad out of control is a disgrace to his mother.

טו שֵׁבֶט וְתוֹכַחַת יִתֵּן חָכְמָה וְנַעַר מְשֻׁלָּח מֵבִישׁ אִמּוֹ:

16 When the wicked increase, offenses increase, But the righteous will see their downfall.

טז בִּרְבוֹת רְשָׁעִים יִרְבֶּה־פָּשַׁע וְצַדִּיקִים בְּמַפַּלְתָּם יִרְאוּ:

17 Discipline your son and he will give you peace; He will gratify you with dainties.

יז יַסֵּר בִּנְךָ וִינִיחֶךָ וְיִתֵּן מַעֲדַנִּים לְנַפְשֶׁךָ:

18 For lack of vision a people lose restraint, But happy is he who heeds instruction.

יח בְּאֵין חָזוֹן יִפָּרַע עָם וְשֹׁמֵר תּוֹרָה אַשְׁרֵהוּ:

19 A slave cannot be disciplined by words; Though he may comprehend, he does not respond.

יט בִּדְבָרִים לֹא־יִוָּסֶר עָבֶד כִּי־יָבִין וְאֵין מַעֲנֶה:

20 If you see a man hasty in speech, There is more hope for a fool than for him.

כ חָזִיתָ אִישׁ אָץ בִּדְבָרָיו תִּקְוָה לִכְסִיל מִמֶּנּוּ:

21 A slave pampered from youth Will come to a bad end.

כא מְפַנֵּק מִנֹּעַר עַבְדּוֹ וְאַחֲרִיתוֹ יִהְיֶה מָנוֹן:

22 An angry man provokes a quarrel; A hot-tempered man commits many offenses.

כב אִישׁ־אַף יְגָרֶה מָדוֹן וּבַעַל חֵמָה רַב־פָּשַׁע:

51

23 A man's pride will humiliate him, But a humble man will obtain honor.

גַּאֲוַת אָדָם תַּשְׁפִּילֶנּוּ וּשְׁפַל־רוּחַ יִתְמֹךְ כָּבוֹד:

ga-a-VAT a-DAM tash-pee-LE-nu ush-fal RU-akh yit-MOKH ka-VOD

24 He who shares with a thief is his own enemy; He hears the imprecation and does not tell.

חוֹלֵק עִם־גַּנָּב שׂוֹנֵא נַפְשׁוֹ אָלָה יִשְׁמַע וְלֹא יַגִּיד:

25 A man's fears become a trap for him, But he who trusts in *Hashem* shall be safeguarded.

חֶרְדַּת אָדָם יִתֵּן מוֹקֵשׁ וּבוֹטֵחַ בַּיהוָה יְשֻׂגָּב:

26 Many seek audience with a ruler, But it is from *Hashem* that a man gets justice.

רַבִּים מְבַקְשִׁים פְּנֵי־מוֹשֵׁל וּמֵיהוָה מִשְׁפַּט־אִישׁ:

27 The unjust man is an abomination to the righteous, And he whose way is straight is an abomination to the wicked.

תּוֹעֲבַת צַדִּיקִים אִישׁ עָוֶל וְתוֹעֲבַת רָשָׁע יְשַׁר־דָּרֶךְ:

30 1 The words of *Agur* son of *Yakeh*, [man of] *Massa*; The speech of the man to *Itiel*, to *Itiel* and *Ukal*:

ל א דִּבְרֵי אָגוּר בִּן־יָקֶה הַמַּשָּׂא נְאֻם הַגֶּבֶר לְאִיתִיאֵל לְאִיתִיאֵל וְאֻכָל:

2 I am brutish, less than a man; I lack common sense.

ב כִּי בַעַר אָנֹכִי מֵאִישׁ וְלֹא־בִינַת אָדָם לִי:

3 I have not learned wisdom, Nor do I possess knowledge of the Holy One.

ג וְלֹא־לָמַדְתִּי חָכְמָה וְדַעַת קְדֹשִׁים אֵדָע:

4 Who has ascended heaven and come down? Who has gathered up the wind in the hollow of his hand? Who has wrapped the waters in his garment? Who has established all the extremities of the earth? What is his name or his son's name, if you know it?

ד מִי עָלָה־שָׁמַיִם וַיֵּרַד מִי אָסַף־רוּחַ בְּחָפְנָיו מִי צָרַר־מַיִם בַּשִּׂמְלָה מִי הֵקִים כָּל־אַפְסֵי־אָרֶץ מַה־שְּׁמוֹ וּמַה־שֶּׁם־בְּנוֹ כִּי תֵדָע:

5 Every word of *Hashem* is pure, A shield to those who take refuge in Him.

ה כָּל־אִמְרַת אֱלוֹהַּ צְרוּפָה מָגֵן הוּא לַחֹסִים בּוֹ:

6 Do not add to His words, Lest He indict you and you be proved a liar.

ו אַל־תּוֹסְףְּ עַל־דְּבָרָיו פֶּן־יוֹכִיחַ בְּךָ וְנִכְזָבְתָּ:

7 Two things I ask of you; do not deny them to me before I die:

ז שְׁתַּיִם שָׁאַלְתִּי מֵאִתָּךְ אַל־תִּמְנַע מִמֶּנִּי בְּטֶרֶם אָמוּת:

8 Keep lies and false words far from me; Give me neither poverty nor riches, But provide me with my daily bread,

ח שָׁוְא וּדְבַר־כָּזָב הַרְחֵק מִמֶּנִּי רֵאשׁ וָעֹשֶׁר אַל־תִּתֶּן־לִי הַטְרִיפֵנִי לֶחֶם חֻקִּי:

SHAV ud-var ka-ZAV har-KHAYK mi-ME-nee RAYSH va-O-sher al TI-ten LEE hat-ree-FAY-nee LE-khem khu-KEE

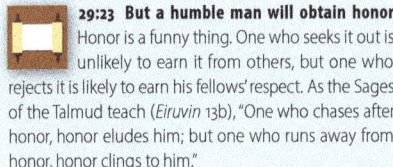

29:23 But a humble man will obtain honor Honor is a funny thing. One who seeks it out is unlikely to earn it from others, but one who rejects it is likely to earn his fellows' respect. As the Sages of the Talmud teach (*Eiruvin* 13b), "One who chases after honor, honor eludes him; but one who runs away from honor, honor clings to him."

30:8 Give me neither poverty nor riches We often think how grateful we would be to have wealth or abundance. This verse points out that often, riches do not lead people to gratitude, but rather to smugness and self-satisfaction. If we have too

The humble acacia tree in the Negev desert

Proverbs

9 Lest, being sated, I renounce, saying, "Who is *Hashem*?" Or, being impoverished, I take to theft And profane the name of my God.

ט פֶּן אֶשְׂבַּע וְכִחַשְׁתִּי וְאָמַרְתִּי מִי יְהֹוָה וּפֶן־אִוָּרֵשׁ וְגָנַבְתִּי וְתָפַשְׂתִּי שֵׁם אֱלֹהָי:

10 Do not inform on a slave to his master, Lest he curse you and you incur guilt.

י אַל־תַּלְשֵׁן עֶבֶד אֶל־אדנו [אֲדֹנָיו] פֶּן־ יְקַלֶּלְךָ וְאָשָׁמְתָּ:

11 There is a breed of men that brings a curse on its fathers And brings no blessing to its mothers,

יא דּוֹר אָבִיו יְקַלֵּל וְאֶת־אִמּוֹ לֹא יְבָרֵךְ:

12 A breed that thinks itself pure, Though it is not washed of its filth;

יב דּוֹר טָהוֹר בְּעֵינָיו וּמִצֹּאָתוֹ לֹא רֻחָץ:

13 A breed so haughty of bearing, so supercilious;

יג דּוֹר מָה־רָמוּ עֵינָיו וְעַפְעַפָּיו יִנָּשֵׂאוּ:

14 A breed whose teeth are swords, Whose jaws are knives, Ready to devour the poor of the land, The needy among men.

יד דּוֹר חֲרָבוֹת שִׁנָּיו וּמַאֲכָלוֹת מְתַלְּעֹתָיו לֶאֱכֹל עֲנִיִּים מֵאֶרֶץ וְאֶבְיוֹנִים מֵאָדָם:

15 The leech has two daughters, "Give!" and "Give!" Three things are insatiable; Four never say, "Enough!":

טו לַעֲלוּקָה שְׁתֵּי בָנוֹת הַב הַב שָׁלוֹשׁ הֵנָּה לֹא תִשְׂבַּעְנָה אַרְבַּע לֹא־אָמְרוּ הוֹן:

16 Sheol, a barren womb, Earth that cannot get enough water, And fire which never says, "Enough!"

טז שְׁאוֹל וְעֹצֶר רָחַם אֶרֶץ לֹא־שָׂבְעָה מַּיִם וְאֵשׁ לֹא־אָמְרָה הוֹן:

17 The eye that mocks a father And disdains the homage due a mother – The ravens of the brook will gouge it out, Young eagles will devour it.

יז עַיִן תִּלְעַג לְאָב וְתָבֻז לִיקֲּהַת־אֵם יִקְּרוּהָ עֹרְבֵי־נַחַל וְיֹאכְלוּהָ בְנֵי־נָשֶׁר:

18 Three things are beyond me; Four I cannot fathom:

יח שְׁלֹשָׁה הֵמָּה נִפְלְאוּ מִמֶּנִּי וארבע [וְאַרְבָּעָה] לֹא יְדַעְתִּים:

19 How an eagle makes its way over the sky; How a snake makes its way over a rock; How a ship makes its way through the high seas; How a man has his way with a maiden.

יט דֶּרֶךְ הַנֶּשֶׁר בַּשָּׁמַיִם דֶּרֶךְ נָחָשׁ עֲלֵי צוּר דֶּרֶךְ־אֳנִיָּה בְלֶב־יָם וְדֶרֶךְ גֶּבֶר בְּעַלְמָה:

20 Such is the way of an adulteress: She eats, wipes her mouth, And says, "I have done no wrong."

כ כֵּן דֶּרֶךְ אִשָּׁה מְנָאָפֶת אָכְלָה וּמָחֲתָה פִיהָ וְאָמְרָה לֹא־פָעַלְתִּי אָוֶן:

21 The earth shudders at three things, At four which it cannot bear:

כא תַּחַת שָׁלוֹשׁ רָגְזָה אֶרֶץ וְתַחַת אַרְבַּע לֹא־תוּכַל שְׂאֵת:

22 A slave who becomes king; A scoundrel sated with food;

כב תַּחַת־עֶבֶד כִּי יִמְלוֹךְ וְנָבָל כִּי יִשְׂבַּע־לָחֶם:

Nahal Dragot in the Judean desert

much of a good thing, we may come to believe we have earned it, and forget *Hashem's* hand in our lives. In fact, the Bible warns that forgetting the Lord and attributing one's wealth to his own power and might is one of the dangers of the blessing of bounty in the Land of Israel (Deuteronomy 8:7–18). Conversely, if we lack something in our lives, we may come to curse God, forgetting He has our best interests at heart. Hence, we should hope to always have just enough for our needs – not to feel the strain of lack, but also not the pride of luxury.

23 A loathsome woman who gets married; A slave-girl who supplants her mistress.

כג תַּחַת שְׂנוּאָה כִּי תִבָּעֵל וְשִׁפְחָה כִּי־תִירַשׁ גְּבִרְתָּהּ:

24 Four are among the tiniest on earth, Yet they are the wisest of the wise:

כד אַרְבָּעָה הֵם קְטַנֵּי־אָרֶץ וְהֵמָּה חֲכָמִים מְחֻכָּמִים:

25 Ants are a folk without power, Yet they prepare food for themselves in summer;

כה הַנְּמָלִים עַם לֹא־עָז וַיָּכִינוּ בַקַּיִץ לַחְמָם:

26 The badger is a folk without strength, Yet it makes its home in the rock;

כו שְׁפַנִּים עַם לֹא־עָצוּם וַיָּשִׂימוּ בַסֶּלַע בֵּיתָם:

27 The locusts have no king, Yet they all march forth in formation;

כז מֶלֶךְ אֵין לָאַרְבֶּה וַיֵּצֵא חֹצֵץ כֻּלּוֹ:

28 You can catch the lizard in your hand, Yet it is found in royal palaces.

כח שְׂמָמִית בְּיָדַיִם תְּתַפֵּשׂ וְהִיא בְּהֵיכְלֵי מֶלֶךְ:

29 There are three that are stately of stride, Four that carry themselves well:

כט שְׁלֹשָׁה הֵמָּה מֵיטִיבֵי צָעַד וְאַרְבָּעָה מֵיטִבֵי לָכֶת:

30 The lion is mightiest among the beasts, And recoils before none;

ל לַיִשׁ גִּבּוֹר בַּבְּהֵמָה וְלֹא־יָשׁוּב מִפְּנֵי־כֹל:

31 The greyhound, the he-goat, The king whom none dares resist.

לא זַרְזִיר מָתְנַיִם אוֹ־תָיִשׁ וּמֶלֶךְ אַלְקוּם עִמּוֹ:

32 If you have been scandalously arrogant, If you have been a schemer, Then clap your hand to your mouth.

לב אִם־נָבַלְתָּ בְהִתְנַשֵּׂא וְאִם־זַמּוֹתָ יָד לְפֶה:

33 As milk under pressure produces butter, And a nose under pressure produces blood, So patience under pressure produces strife.

לג כִּי מִיץ חָלָב יוֹצִיא חֶמְאָה וּמִיץ־אַף יוֹצִיא דָם וּמִיץ אַפַּיִם יוֹצִיא רִיב:

31 1 The words of *Lemuel*, king of Massa, with which his mother admonished him:

לא א דִּבְרֵי לְמוּאֵל מֶלֶךְ מַשָּׂא אֲשֶׁר־יִסְּרַתּוּ אִמּוֹ:

2 No, my son! No, O son of my womb! No, O son of my vows!

ב מַה־בְּרִי וּמַה־בַּר־בִּטְנִי וּמֶה בַּר־נְדָרָי:

3 Do not give your strength to women, Your vigor, to those who destroy kings.

ג אַל־תִּתֵּן לַנָּשִׁים חֵילֶךָ וּדְרָכֶיךָ לַמְחוֹת מְלָכִין:

4 Wine is not for kings, O *Lemuel*; Not for kings to drink, Nor any strong drink for princes,

ד אַל לַמְלָכִים לְמוֹאֵל אַל לַמְלָכִים שְׁתוֹ־יָיִן וּלְרוֹזְנִים אוֹ [אֵי] שֵׁכָר:

5 Lest they drink and forget what has been ordained, And infringe on the rights of the poor.

ה פֶּן־יִשְׁתֶּה וְיִשְׁכַּח מְחֻקָּק וִישַׁנֶּה דִּין כָּל־בְּנֵי־עֹנִי:

6 Give strong drink to the hapless And wine to the embittered.

ו תְּנוּ־שֵׁכָר לְאוֹבֵד וְיַיִן לְמָרֵי נָפֶשׁ:

7 Let them drink and forget their poverty, And put their troubles out of mind.

ז יִשְׁתֶּה וְיִשְׁכַּח רִישׁוֹ וַעֲמָלוֹ לֹא יִזְכָּר־עוֹד:

8 Speak up for the dumb, For the rights of all the unfortunate.

ח פְּתַח־פִּיךָ לְאִלֵּם אֶל־דִּין כָּל־בְּנֵי חֲלוֹף:

Proverbs

9 Speak up, judge righteously, Champion the poor and the needy.

ט פְּתַח־פִּיךָ שְׁפָט־צֶדֶק וְדִין עָנִי וְאֶבְיוֹן:

10 What a rare find is a capable wife! Her worth is far beyond that of rubies.

י אֵשֶׁת־חַיִל מִי יִמְצָא וְרָחֹק מִפְּנִינִים מִכְרָהּ:

AY-shet KHA-yil MEE yim-TZA v'-ra-KHOK mi-p'-nee-NEEM mikh-RAH

11 Her husband puts his confidence in her, And lacks no good thing.

יא בָּטַח בָּהּ לֵב בַּעְלָהּ וְשָׁלָל לֹא יֶחְסָר:

12 She is good to him, never bad, All the days of her life.

יב גְּמָלַתְהוּ טוֹב וְלֹא־רָע כֹּל יְמֵי חַיֶּיהָ:

13 She looks for wool and flax, And sets her hand to them with a will.

יג דָּרְשָׁה צֶמֶר וּפִשְׁתִּים וַתַּעַשׂ בְּחֵפֶץ כַּפֶּיהָ:

14 She is like a merchant fleet, Bringing her food from afar.

יד הָיְתָה כָּאֳנִיּוֹת סוֹחֵר מִמֶּרְחָק תָּבִיא לַחְמָהּ:

15 She rises while it is still night, And supplies provisions for her household, The daily fare of her maids.

טו וַתָּקָם בְּעוֹד לַיְלָה וַתִּתֵּן טֶרֶף לְבֵיתָהּ וְחֹק לְנַעֲרֹתֶיהָ:

16 She sets her mind on an estate and acquires it; She plants a vineyard by her own labors.

טז זָמְמָה שָׂדֶה וַתִּקָּחֵהוּ מִפְּרִי כַפֶּיהָ נטע [נָטְעָה] כָּרֶם:

17 She girds herself with strength, And performs her tasks with vigor.

יז חָגְרָה בְעוֹז מָתְנֶיהָ וַתְּאַמֵּץ זְרוֹעֹתֶיהָ:

18 She sees that her business thrives; Her lamp never goes out at night.

יח טָעֲמָה כִּי־טוֹב סַחְרָהּ לֹא־יִכְבֶּה בליל [בַלַּיְלָה] נֵרָהּ:

19 She sets her hand to the distaff; Her fingers work the spindle.

יט יָדֶיהָ שִׁלְּחָה בַכִּישׁוֹר וְכַפֶּיהָ תָּמְכוּ פָלֶךְ:

20 She gives generously to the poor; Her hands are stretched out to the needy.

כ כַּפָּהּ פָּרְשָׂה לֶעָנִי וְיָדֶיהָ שִׁלְּחָה לָאֶבְיוֹן:

21 She is not worried for her household because of snow, For her whole household is dressed in crimson.

כא לֹא־תִירָא לְבֵיתָהּ מִשָּׁלֶג כִּי כָל־בֵּיתָהּ לָבֻשׁ שָׁנִים:

22 She makes covers for herself; Her clothing is linen and purple.

כב מַרְבַדִּים עָשְׂתָה־לָּהּ שֵׁשׁ וְאַרְגָּמָן לְבוּשָׁהּ:

31:10 A capable wife This chapter contains an extended poem in praise of the *eishet chayil*, translated here as 'capable wife,' but generally referred to as the 'woman of valor' (verses 10–31). She provides for her family in all ways, both materially and spiritually, and her endeavors and accomplishments are praised by the members of her household and by others. This poem is sung by Jews around the world on Friday nights, as they begin the first *Shabbat* meal. It is often understood as a praise for the Jewish woman who works hard to care for her family and for others, and to prepare for the *Shabbat* each week. On a more mystical plane, it has been said in the name of the sixteenth century Kabbalist Rabbi Yitzchak Luria, who is known by the acronym *Arizal*, that "the Land of Israel is the earthly manifestation of the woman of valor." When the Children of Israel follow *Hashem* faithfully in this unique land, they are provided for, both materially and spiritually. And, the beauty and charm of *Eretz Yisrael* are recognized and praised by all, Jews and non-Jews alike.

Three-jet waterfall in Northern Israel

23 Her husband is prominent in the gates, As he sits among the elders of the land.

נוֹדָע בַּשְּׁעָרִים בַּעְלָהּ בְּשִׁבְתּוֹ עִם־זִקְנֵי־ אָרֶץ: כג

24 She makes cloth and sells it, And offers a girdle to the merchant.

סָדִין עָשְׂתָה וַתִּמְכֹּר וַחֲגוֹר נָתְנָה לַכְּנַעֲנִי: כד

25 She is clothed with strength and splendor; She looks to the future cheerfully.

עֹז־וְהָדָר לְבוּשָׁהּ וַתִּשְׂחַק לְיוֹם אַחֲרוֹן: כה

26 Her mouth is full of wisdom, Her tongue with kindly teaching.

פִּיהָ פָּתְחָה בְחָכְמָה וְתוֹרַת־חֶסֶד עַל־ לְשׁוֹנָהּ: כו

27 She oversees the activities of her household And never eats the bread of idleness.

צוֹפִיָּה הֲלִיכוֹת בֵּיתָהּ וְלֶחֶם עַצְלוּת לֹא תֹאכֵל: כז

28 Her children declare her happy; Her husband praises her,

קָמוּ בָנֶיהָ וַיְאַשְּׁרוּהָ בַּעְלָהּ וַיְהַלְלָהּ: כח

29 "Many women have done well, But you surpass them all."

רַבּוֹת בָּנוֹת עָשׂוּ חָיִל וְאַתְּ עָלִית עַל־ כֻּלָּנָה: כט

30 Grace is deceptive, Beauty is illusory; It is for her fear of *Hashem* That a woman is to be praised.

שֶׁקֶר הַחֵן וְהֶבֶל הַיֹּפִי אִשָּׁה יִרְאַת־יְהֹוָה הִיא תִתְהַלָּל: ל

31 Extol her for the fruit of her hand, And let her works praise her in the gates.

תְּנוּ־לָהּ מִפְּרִי יָדֶיהָ וִיהַלְלוּהָ בַשְּׁעָרִים מַעֲשֶׂיהָ: לא

List of Transliterated Words in *The Israel Bible*

The following is a list of nouns which have been transliterated into Hebrew in the English translation and commentary of *The Israel Bible*:

Hebrew Name	English Name	Pronunciation	Hebrew
Achan	Achan	a-KHAN	עָכָן
Achav	Ahab	akh-AV	אַחְאָב
Achaz	Ahaz	a-KHAZ	אָחָז
Achazyahu	Ahaziah	a-khaz-YA-hu	אֲחַזְיָהוּ
Achiezer	Ahiezer	a-khee-E-zer	אֲחִיעֶזֶר
Achihud	Ahihud	a-khee-HUD	אֲחִיהוּד
Achikam	Ahikam	a-khee-KAM	אֲחִיקָם
Achilud	Ahilud	a-khee-LUD	אֲחִילוּד
Achimelech	Ahimelech	a-khee-ME-lekh	אֲחִימֶלֶךְ
Achira	Ahira	a-khee-RA	אֲחִירַע
Achisamach	Ahisamach	a-khee-sa-MAKH	אֲחִיסָמָךְ
Achitofel	Ahithophel	a-khee-TO-fel	אֲחִיתֹפֶל
Achituv	Ahitub	a-khee-TUV	אֲחִיטוּב
Achiya	Ahijah	a-khi-YAH	אֲחִיָּה
Adam	Adam	a-DAM	אָדָם
Adar	Adar	a-DAR	אֲדָר
Adoniyahu	Adonijah	a-do-ni-YA-hu	אֲדֹנִיָּהוּ
Adulam	Adullam	a-du-LAM	עֲדֻלָּם
Agur	Agur	a-GUR	אָגוּר
Aharon	Aaron	a-ha-RON	אַהֲרֹן
Amasa	Amasa	a-ma-SA	עֲמָשָׂא
Amatzya	Amaziah	a-matz-YAH	אֲמַצְיָה
Amen	Amen	a-MAYN	אָמֵן
Amiel	Ammiel	a-mee-AYL	עַמִּיאֵל
Aminadav	Amminadab	a-mee-na-DAV	עַמִּינָדָב
Amitai	Amittai	a-mi-TAI	אֲמִתַּי
Amnon	Amnon	am-NON	אַמְנוֹן

Hebrew Name	English Name	Pronunciation	Hebrew
Amon	Amon	a-MON	אָמוֹן
Amos	Amos	a-MOS	עָמוֹס
Amotz	Amoz	a-MOTZ	אָמוֹץ
Amram	Amram	am-RAM	עַמְרָם
Anatot	Anathoth	a-na-TOT	עֲנָתוֹת
Aron	Ark	a-RON	אֲרוֹן
Aron HaBrit	Ark of the Covenant	a-RON ha-b'-REET	אֲרוֹן הַבְּרִית
Arpachshad	Arpachshad	ar-pakh-SHAD	אַרְפַּכְשַׁד
Asa	Asa	a-SA	אָסָא
Asael	Asahel	a-sah-AYL	עֲשָׂהאֵל
Asaf	Asaph	a-SAF	אָסָף
Ashdod	Ashdod	ash-DOD	אַשְׁדּוֹד
Asher	Asher	a-SHAYR	אָשֵׁר
Ashkelon	Ashkelon	ash-k'-LON	אַשְׁקְלוֹן
Atalya	Athaliah	a-tal-YAH	עֲתַלְיָה
Avdon	Abdon	av-DON	עַבְדּוֹן
Avichayil	Abihail	a-vee-KHA-yil	אֲבִיחַיִל
Avidan	Abidan	a-vee-DAN	אֲבִידָן
Avigail	Abigail	a-vee-GA-yil	אֲבִיגַיִל
Avihu	Abihu	a-vee-HU	אֲבִיהוּא
Avimelech	Abimelech	a-vee-ME-lekh	אֲבִימֶלֶךְ
Avinadav	Abinadab	a-vee-na-DAV	אֲבִינָדָב
Aviram	Abiram	a-vee-RAM	אֲבִירָם
Avishai	Abishai	a-vee-SHAI	אֲבִישַׁי
Aviya	Abijah	a-vi-YAH	אֲבִיָּה
Aviyam	Abijam	a-vi-YAM	אֲבִיָּם
Avner	Abner	av-NAYR	אַבְנֵר
Avraham	Abraham	av-ra-HAM	אַבְרָהָם
Avram	Abram	av-RAM	אַבְרָם
Avshalom	Absalom	av-sha-LOM	אַבְשָׁלוֹם
Azarya	Azariah	a-zar-YAH	עֲזַרְיָה
Azeika	Azekah	a-zay-KAH	עֲזֵקָה
Azza	Gaza	a-ZAH	עַזָּה

Hebrew Name	English Name	Pronunciation	Hebrew
B'nei Yisrael	The Children of Israel	b'-NAY yis-ra-AYL	בְּנֵי יִשְׂרָאֵל
Barak	Barak	ba-rakh-AYL	בָּרָק
Baruch	Baruch	ba-RUKH	בָּרוּךְ
Barzilai	Barzillai	bar-zi-LAI	בַּרְזִלַּי
Basha	Baasa	ba-SHA	בַּעְשָׁא
Batsheva	Bath-sheba	bat-SHE-va	בַּת־שֶׁבַע
Be'er Sheva	Beer-sheba	b'-AYR SHE-va	בְּאֵר שֶׁבַע
Be'eri	Beeri	b'-ay-REE	בְּאֵרִי
Beit Aven	Beth-aven	bayt A-ven	בֵּית אָוֶן
Beit El	Beth-el	bayt el	בֵּית אֵל
Beit Hamikdash	Temple	bayt ha-mik-DASH	בֵּית הַמִּקְדָּשׁ
Beit Lechem	Beth-lehem	bayt LE-khem	בֵּית לֶחֶם
Beit Shean	Beth-shean	bayt sh'-AN	בֵּית שְׁאָן
Beit Shemesh	Beth-shemesh	bayt SHE-mesh	בֵּית שֶׁמֶשׁ
Berechya	Berechiah	be-rekh-YAH	בֶּרֶכְיָה
Betzalel	Bezalel	b'-tzal-AYL	בְּצַלְאֵל
Bilha	Bilhah	bil-HAH	בִּלְהָה
Binyamin	Benjamin	bin-ya-MIN	בִּנְיָמִין
Boaz	Boaz	BO-az	בֹּעַז
Buki	Bukki	bu-KEE	בֻּקִּי
Buzi	Buzi	bu-ZEE	בּוּזִי
Carmel	Carmel	kar-MEL	כַּרְמֶל
Chachalya	Hacaliah	kha-khal-YAH	חֲכַלְיָה
Chagai	Haggai	kha-GAI	חַגִּי
Chana	Hannah	kha-NAH	חַנָּה
Chanamel	Hanamel	kha-nam-AYL	חֲנַמְאֵל
Chanani	Hanani	kha-NA-nee	חֲנָנִי
Chananya	Hananiah	kha-nan-YAH	חֲנַנְיָה
Chaniel	Hanniel	kha-nee-AYL	חַנִּיאֵל
Chanoch	Enoch	kha-NOKH	חֲנוֹךְ
Chava	Eve	kha-VAH	חַוָּה
Chavakuk	Habakkuk	kha-va-KUK	חֲבַקּוּק
Chermon	Hermon	kher-MON	חֶרְמוֹן

Hebrew Name	English Name	Pronunciation	Hebrew
Chetzron	Hezron	khetz-RON	חֶצְרוֹן
Chever	Heber	KHE-ver	חֶבֶר
Chevron	Hebron	khev-RON	חֶבְרוֹן
Chilkiyahu	Hilkiah	khil-ki-YA-hu	חִלְקִיָּהוּ
Chizkiyahu	Hezekiah	khiz-ki-YA-hu	חִזְקִיָּהוּ
Chofni	Hophni	khof-NEE	חָפְנִי
Chogla	Hoglah	khog-LAH	חָגְלָה
Chulda	Hulda	khul-DAH	חֻלְדָּה
Chur	Hur	Khur	חוּר
Dan	Dan	Dan	דָּן
Daniel	Daniel	da-ni-YAYL	דָּנִיֵּאל
Datan	Dathan	da-TAN	דָּתָן
David	David	da-VID	דָּוִד
Devora	Deborah	d'-vo-RAH	דְּבוֹרָה
Dina	Dinah	DEE-nah	דִּינָה
Doeg Ha'adomi	Doeg the Edomite	do-AYG ha-a-do-MEE	דּוֹאֵג הָאֲדֹמִי
Efraim	Ephraim	ef-RA-yim	אֶפְרַיִם
Efrat	Ephrat	ef-RAT	אֶפְרָתָה
Efrat	Ephrathah	ef-RA-tah	אֶפְרָתָה
Ehud	Ehud	ay-HUD	אֵהוּד
Eila	Elah	AY-lah	אֵלָה
Eilon	Elon	ay-LON	אֵילוֹן
Ein Gedi	En-gedi	ayn GE-dee	עֵין גֶּדִי
Elazar	Eleazar	el-a-ZAR	אֶלְעָזָר
Elchanan	Elhanan	el-kha-NAN	אֶלְחָנָן
Eli	Eli	ay-LEE	עֵלִי
Eliav	Eliab	e-lee-AV	אֱלִיאָב
Elidad	Elidad	e-lee-DAD	אֱלִידָד
Eliezer	Eliezer	e-lee-E-zer	אֱלִיעֶזֶר
Elimelech	Elimelech	e-lee-ME-lekh	אֱלִימֶלֶךְ
Elisha	Elisha	e-lee-SHA	אֱלִישָׁע
Elishama	Elishama	e-lee-sha-MA	אֱלִישָׁמָע
Elisheva	Elisheba	e-lee-SHE-va	אֱלִישֶׁבַע

Hebrew Name	English Name	Pronunciation	Hebrew
Elitzafan	Eli-zaphan	e-lee-tza-FAN	אֱלִיצָפָן
Elitzur	Elizur	e-lee-TZUR	אֱלִיצוּר
Eliyahu	Elijah	ay-li-YA-hu	אֵלִיָּהוּ
Elkana	Elkanah	el-ka-NAH	אֶלְקָנָה
Elyasaf	Eliasaph	el-ya-SAF	אֶלְיָסָף
Elyashiv	Eliashib	el-ya-SHEEV	אֶלְיָשִׁיב
Enosh	Enosh	e-NOSH	אֱנוֹשׁ
Er	Er	ayr	עֵר
Eshtaol	Eshtaol	esh-ta-OL	אֶשְׁתָּאֹל
Esther	Esther	es-TAYR	אֶסְתֵּר
Eved Melech	Ebed-melech	E-ved ME-lekh	עֶבֶד־מֶלֶךְ
Even Ha-Ezer	Eben-Ezer	E-ven ha-E-zer	אֶבֶן הָעֵזֶר
Ever	Eber	AY-ver	עֵבֶר
Evyatar	Abiathar	ev-ya-TAR	אֶבְיָתָר
Ezra	Ezra	ez-RA	עֶזְרָא
Gad	Gad	gad	גָּד
Gadi	Gaddi	ga-DEE	גַּדִּי
Gadiel	Gaddiel	ga-dee-AYL	גַּדִּיאֵל
Gamliel	Gamaliel	gam-lee-AYL	גַּמְלִיאֵל
Gedalia	Gedaliah	g'-dal-YA (hu)	גְּדַלְיָהוּ
Gedera	Gederah	g'-day-RAH	גְּדֵרָה
Gershom	Gershom	gay-r'-SHOM	גֵּרְשׁוֹם
Gershon	Gershon	gay-r'-SHON	גֵּרְשׁוֹן
Geshem	Geshem	GE-shem	גֶּשֶׁם
Geuel	Geuel	g'-u-AYL	גְּאוּאֵל
Gidon	Gideon	gid-ON	גִּדְעוֹן
Gilad	Gilead	gil-AD	גִּלְעָד
Gilgal	Gilgal	gil-GAL	גִּלְגָּל
Giva	Gibeah	giv-AH	גִּבְעָה
Givon	Gibeon	giv-ON	גִּבְעוֹן
Hadassa	Hadassah	ha-da-SAH	הֲדַסָּה
Har Eival	Mount Ebal	ay-VAL	הַר עֵיבָל
Har Gerizim	Mount Gerizim	g'-ri-ZEEM	הַר גְּרִזִים

Hebrew Name	English Name	Pronunciation	Hebrew
Har HaBayit	Temple Mount	har ha-BA-yit	הַר הַבַּיִת
Har HaZeitim	the Mount of Olives	har ha-zay-TEEM	הַר הַזֵּיתִים
Hashem	Lord/God		
Hayman	Heman	hay-MAN	הֵימָן
Hoshea	Hosea	ho-SHAY-a	הוֹשֵׁעַ
Ido	Iddo	i-DO	עִדּוֹ
Imanu-El	Immanuel	i-MA-nu ayl	עִמָּנוּ אֵל
Ish-boshet	Ish-bosheth	eesh BO-shet	אִישׁ־בֹּשֶׁת
Itamar	Ithamar	ee-ta-MAR	אִיתָמָר
Itiel	Ithiel	ee-tee-AYL	אִיתִיאֵל
Ivtzan	Ibzan	iv-TZAN	אִבְצָן
Iyov	Job	i-YOV	אִיּוֹב
Kadmiel	Kadmiel	kad-mee-AYL	קַדְמִיאֵל
Kalev	Caleb	ka-LAYV	כָּלֵב
Keesh	Kish	keesh	קִישׁ
Kehat	Kohath	k'-HAT	קְהָת
Keinan	Kenan	kay-NAN	קֵינָן
Kemuel	Kemuel	k'-mu-AYL	קְמוּאֵל
Keruvim	Cherubim	k'-ru-VEEM	כְּרוּבִים
Kilyon	Chilion	kil-YON	כִּלְיוֹן
Kiryat Arba	Kiriath-arba	keer-YAT AR-bah	קִרְיַת אַרְבַּע
Kiryat Sefer	Kiriath-sepher	keer-YAT SAY-fer	קִרְיַת־סֵפֶר
Kiryat Ye'arim	Kiriath-jearim	keer-YAT y'-a-REEM	קִרְיַת יְעָרִים
Kislev	Chislev	kis-LAYV	כִּסְלֵו
Kohanim	Priests	ko-ha-NEEM	כֹּהֲנִים
Kohelet	Koheleth	ko-HE-let	קֹהֶלֶת
Kohen	Priest	ko-HAYN	כֹּהֵן
Kohen Gadol	High Priest	ko-HAYN ga-DOL	כֹּהֵן גָּדוֹל
Korach	Korah	KO-rakh	קֹרַח
Kushi	Cushi	ku-SHEE	כּוּשִׁי
Lachish	Lachish	la-KHEESH	לָכִישׁ
Leah	Leah	lay-AH	לֵאָה
Lemech	Lamech	LE-mekh	לֶמֶךְ

Hebrew Name	English Name	Pronunciation	Hebrew
Lemuel	Lemuel	l'-mu-AYL	לְמוּאֵל
Levi	Levi	lay-VEE	לֵוִי
Leviim	Levites	l'-vee-IM	לְוִים
Machla	Mahlah	makh-LAH	מַחְלָה
Machlon	Mahlon	makh-LON	מַחְלוֹן
Machseya	Mahseiah	makh-say-YAH	מַחְסֵיָה
Malachi	Malachi	mal-a-KHEE	מַלְאָכִי
Manoach	Manoah	ma-NO-akh	מָנוֹחַ
Mashiach	Messiah	ma-SHEE-akh	מָשִׁיחַ
Mefiboshet	Mephibosheth	m'-fee-VO-shet	מְפִיבֹשֶׁת
Mehalalel	Mahalalel	ma-ha-lal-AYL	מַהֲלַלְאֵל
Menachem	Menahem	m'-na-KHAYM	מְנַחֵם
Menashe	Menasseh	m'-na-SHEH	מְנַשֶּׁה
Menorah	Candlestick	m'-no-RAH	מְנֹרָה
Merari	Merari	m'-ra-REE	מְרָרִי
Metushelach	Methusaleh	m'-tu-SHE-lakh	מְתוּשֶׁלַח
Micha	Micah	mee-KHAH	מִיכָה
Michael	Michael	mee-kha-AYL	מִיכָאֵל
Michaihu	Micaiah	mee-KHAI-hu	מִיכָיְהוּ
Michal	Michal	mee-KHAL	מִיכַל
Milka	Milcah	mil-KAH	מִלְכָּה
Miriam	Miriam	mir-YAM	מִרְיָם
Mishael	Mishael	mee-sha-AYL	מִישָׁאֵל
Mishkan	Tabernacle	mish-KAN	מִשְׁכָּן
Mitzpa	Mizpah	mitz-PAH	מִצְפָּה
Mizbayach	Altar	miz-BAY-akh	מִזְבֵּחַ
Mordechai	Mordecai	mor-d'-KHAI	מָרְדֳּכַי
Moriah	Moriah	mo-ri-YAH	מוֹרִיָּה
Moshe	Moses	mo-SHEH	מֹשֶׁה
Nachbi	Nahbi	nakh-BEE	נַחְבִּי
Nachor	Nahor	na-KHOR	נָחוֹר
Nachshon	Nahshon	nakh-SHON	נַחְשׁוֹן
Nachum	Nahum	na-KHUM	נַחוּם

Hebrew Name	English Name	Pronunciation	Hebrew
Nadav	Nadab	na-DAV	נָדָב
Naftali	Naphtali	naf-ta-LEE	נַפְתָּלִי
Naomi	Naomi	na-o-MEE	נָעֳמִי
Natan	Nathan	na-TAN	נָתָן
Naval	Nabal	na-VAL	נָבָל
Navi	Prophet	na-VEE	נָבִיא
Navot	Naboth	na-VAL	נָבָל
Nechemya	Nehemiah	n'-khem-YAH	נְחֶמְיָה
Negev	Negeb	NE-gev	נֶגֶב
Nerya	Neriah	nay-ri-YAH	נֵרִיָּה
Netanel	Nethanel	n'-tan-AYL	נְתַנְאֵל
Neviah	Prophetess	n'-vee-AH	נְבִיאָה
Neviim	Prophets	n'-vee-EEM	נְבִיאִים
Nisan	Nisan	nee-SAN	נִיסָן
Noa	Noah	no-AH	נֹעָה
Noach	Noah	NO-akh	נֹחַ
Nov	Nob	nov	נֹב
Nun	Nun	nun	נוּן
Oded	Oded	o-DAYD	עוֹדֵד
Ohola	Oholah	a-ho-LAH	אָהֳלָה
Oholiav	Oholiab	o-ha-lee-AV	אָהֳלִיאָב
Oholiva	Oholibah	a-ho-lee-VAH	אָהֳלִיבָה
Omri	Omri	om-REE	עָמְרִי
Onan	Onan	o-NAN	אוֹנָן
Otniel	Othniel	ot-nee-AYL	עָתְנִיאֵל
Ovadya	Obadiah	o-vad-YAH	עֹבַדְיָה
Oved	Obed	o-VAYD	עוֹבֵד
Oved Edom	Obed Edom	o-VAYD e-DOM	עוֹבֵד אֱדוֹם
Pagiel	Pagiel	pag-ee-AYL	פַּגְעִיאֵל
Palti	Palti	pal-TEE	פַּלְטִי
Paltiel	Paltiel	pal-tee-AYL	פַּלְטִיאֵל
Pekach	Pekah	PE-kakh	פֶּקַח
Pedael	Pedahel	p'-da-AYL	פְּדַהְאֵל

64

Hebrew Name	English Name	Pronunciation	Hebrew
Pekachya	Pekahiah	p'-kakh-YAH	פְּקַחְיָה
Peleg	Peleg	PE-leg	פֶּלֶג
Penina	Peninnah	p'-ni-NAH	פְּנִנָּה
Peretz	Perez	PE-retz	פֶּרֶץ
Petuel	Pethuel	p'-tu-AYL	פְּתוּאֵל
Pinchas	Phinehas	peen-KHAS	פִּינְחָס
Rachel	Rachel	ra-KHAYL	רָחֵל
Ram	Ram	ram	רָם
Rama	Ramah	ra-MAH	רָמָה
Re'u	Reu	r'-U	רְעוּ
Rechovam	Rehoboam	r'-khav-AM	רְחַבְעָם
Reuven	Reuben	r'-u-VAYN	רְאוּבֵן
Rivka	Rebecca	riv-KAH	רִבְקָה
Rut	Ruth	rut	רוּת
Salma	Salmon/Salmah	sal-MAH	שַׂלְמָה
Salmon	Salmon	sal-MON	שַׂלְמוֹן
Sara	Sarah	sa-RAH	שָׂרָה
Sarai	Sarai	sa-RAI	שָׂרַי
Selah	Selah	SE-lah	סֶלָה
Seraya	Seraiah	s'-ra-YAH	שְׂרָיָה
Serug	Serug	s'-RUG	שְׂרוּג
Setur	Sethur	s'-TUR	סְתוּר
Shaarayim	Shaaraim	sha-a-RA-yim	שַׁעֲרַיִם
Shabbat	Sabbath	sha-BAT	שַׁבָּת
Shabbatot	Sabbaths	sha-ba-TOT	שַׁבָּתוֹת
Shafan	Shaphan	sha-FAN	שָׁפָן
Shafat	Shaphat	sha-FAT	שָׁפָט
Shalem	Salem	sha-LAYM	שָׁלֵם
Shalum	Shallum	sha-LUM	שַׁלּוּם
Shamgar	Shamgar	sham-GAR	שַׁמְגַּר
Shamua	Shammua	sha-MU-a	שַׁמּוּעַ
Shaul	Saul	sha-UL	שָׁאוּל
Shealtiel	Shealtiel	sh'-al-tee-AYL	שְׁאַלְתִּיאֵל

Hebrew Name	English Name	Pronunciation	Hebrew
Shear Yashuv	Shear-Jashub	sh'-AR ya-SHUV	שְׁאָר יָשׁוּב
Shechanya	Shecaniah	sh'-khan-YAH	שְׁכַנְיָה
Shechem	Shechem	sh'-KHEM	שְׁכֶם
Sheila	Shelah	shay-LAH	שֵׁלָה
Shelach	Shelah	SHE-lakh	שֶׁלַח
Shelumiel	Shelumiel	sh'-lu-mee-AYL	שְׁלֻמִיאֵל
Shem	Shem	Shaym	שֵׁם
Shemaya	Shemaiah	sh'-ma-YAH	שְׁמַעְיָה
Sheshbatzar	Sheshbazzar	shaysh-ba-TZAR	שֵׁשְׁבַּצַּר
Shet	Seth	Shayt	שֵׁת
Shevat	Shebat	sh'-VAT	שְׁבָט
Shilo	Shiloh	shi-LOH	שִׁלֹה
Shim'i	Shimei	shim-EE	שִׁמְעִי
Shimon	Simeon	shim-ON	שִׁמְעוֹן
Shimshon	Samson	shim-SHON	שִׁמְשׁוֹן
Shlomo	Solomon	sh'-lo-MOH	שְׁלֹמֹה
Shmuel	Samuel	sh'-mu-AYL	שְׁמוּאֵל
Shofar	Horn	sho-FAR	שׁוֹפָר
Shofarot	Horns	sho-fa-ROT	שׁוֹפָרוֹת
Shomron	Samaria	sho-m'-RON	שֹׁמְרוֹן
Sivan	Sivan	see-VAN	סִיוָן
Tamar	Tamar	ta-MAR	תָּמָר
Tanakh	Hebrew Bible	ta-NAKH	תָּנָ"ךְ
Tapuach	Tappuah	ta-PU-akh	תַּפּוּחַ
Tavor	Tabor	ta-VOR	תָּבוֹר
Tekoa	Tekoa	t'-KO-a	תְּקוֹעַה
Terach	Terah	TE-rakh	תֶּרַח
Teveria	Tiberias	t'-ver-YAH	טְבֶרְיָה
Tevet	Tebeth	tay-VAYT	טֵבֵת
Tirtza	Tirzah	tir-TZAH	תִּרְצָה
Tola	Tola	to-LA	תּוֹלָע
Tzadok	Zadok	tza-DOK	צָדוֹק
Tzefanya	Zephaniah	tz'-fan-YAH	צְפַנְיָה

Hebrew Name	English Name	Pronunciation	Hebrew
Tzelofchad	Zelophehad	tz'-lo-f-KHAD	צְלָפְחָד
Tzeruya	Zeruiah	tz'-ru-YAH	צְרוּיָה
Tzfat	Safed	tz'-FAT	צְפַת
Tzidkiyahu	Zedekiah	tzid-ki-YA-hu	צִדְקִיָּהוּ
Tziklag	Ziklag	tzi-k'-LAG	צִקְלָג
Tzion	Zion	tzi-YON	צִיּוֹן
Tzipora	Zipporah	tzi-po-RAH	צִפֹּרָה
Tzora	Zorah	tzor-AH	צָרְעָה
Tzuriel	Zuriel	tzu-ree-AYL	צוּרִיאֵל
Ukal	Ucal	u-KAL	אֻכָל
Uri	Uri	u-REE	אוּרִי
Uriya	Uriah	u-ri-YAH	אוּרִיָּה
Utz	Uz	Utz	עוּץ
Uzziyahu	Uzziah	u-zi-YA-hu	עֻזִּיָּהוּ
Yaakov	Jacob	ya-a-KOV	יַעֲקֹב
Yachaziel	Jahaziel	ya-kha-zee-AYL	יַחֲזִיאֵל
Yael	Jael	ya-AYL	יָעֵל
Yaffo	Joppa/Jaffa	ya-FO	יָפוֹ
Yair	Jair	ya-EER	יָאִיר
Yakeh	Jakeh	ya-KEH	יָקֶה
Yarden	Jordan	yar-DAYN	יַרְדֵּן
Yarmut	Jarmuth	yar-MUT	יַרְמוּת
Yechezkel	Ezekiel	y'-khez-KAYL	יְחֶזְקֵאל
Yechiel	Jehiel	y'-khee-AYL	יְחִיאֵל
Yechonya	Jeconiah	y'-khon-YAH	יְכָנְיָה
Yedutun	Jeduthun	y'-du-TUN	יְדוּתוּן
Yehoachaz	Jehoahaz	y'-ho-a-KHAZ	יְהוֹאָחָז
Yehoash	Jehoash	y'-ho-ASH	יְהוֹאָשׁ
Yehochanan	Jehohanan	y'-ho-kha-NAN	יְהוֹחָנָן
Yehonatan	Jonathan	y'-ho-na-TAN	יְהוֹנָתָן
Yehoram	Jehoram	y'-ho-RAM	יְהוֹרָם
Yehoshafat	Jehoshaphat	y'-ho-sha-FAT	יְהוֹשָׁפָט
Yehoshavat	Jehoshabeath	y'-ho-shav-AT	יְהוֹשַׁבְעַת

Hebrew Name	English Name	Pronunciation	Hebrew
Yehosheva	Jehosheba	y-ho-SHE-va	יְהוֹשֶׁבַע
Yehoshua	Joshua	y'-ho-SHU-a	יְהוֹשֻׁעַ
Yehotzadak	Jehozadak	y'-ho-tza-DAK	יְהוֹצָדָק
Yehoyachin	Jehoiachin	y'-ho-ya-KHEEN	יְהוֹיָכִין
Yehoyada	Jehoiada	y'-ho-ya-DA	יְהוֹיָדָע
Yehoyakim	Jehoiakim	y'-ho-ya-KEEM	יְהוֹיָקִים
Yehu	Jehu	yay-HU	יֵהוּא
Yehuda	Judah	y'-hu-DAH	יְהוּדָה
Yehudi	Jew	y'-hu-DEE	יְהוּדִי
Yehudim	Jews	y'-hu-DEEM	יְהוּדִים
Yered	Jared	YE-red	יֶרֶד
Yericho	Jericho	y'-ree-KHO	יְרִיחוֹ
Yerovam	Jeroboam	ya-rov-AM	יָרָבְעָם
Yerubaal	Jerubbaal	y'-ru-BA-al	יְרֻבַּעַל
Yerushalayim	Jerusalem	y'-ru-sha-LA-yim	יְרוּשָׁלַיִם
Yeshayahu	Isaiah	y'-sha-YA-hu	יְשַׁעְיָהוּ
Yeshua	Jeshua	yay-SHU-a	יֵשׁוּעַ
Yiftach	Jephthah	yif-TAKH	יִפְתָּח
Yigal	Igal	yig-AL	יִגְאָל
Yirmiyahu	Jeremiah	yir-m'-YA-hu	יִרְמְיָהוּ
Yishai	Jesse	yi-SHAI	יִשַׁי
Yisrael	Israel	yis-ra-AYL	יִשְׂרָאֵל
Yissachar	Issachar	yi-sa-KHAR	יִשָּׂשכָר
Yitzchak	Issac	yitz-KHAK	יִצְחָק
Yizrael	Jezreel	yiz-r'-EL	יִזְרְעָאל
Yoash	Joash	yo-ASH	יוֹאָשׁ
Yoav	Joab	yo-AV	יוֹאָב
Yochanan	Johanan	yo-kha-NAN	יוֹחָנָן
Yocheved	Jochebed	yo-KHE-ved	יוֹכֶבֶד
Yoel	Joel	yo-AYL	יוֹאֵל
Yona	Jonah	yo-NAH	יוֹנָה
Yonadav	Jonadab	yo-na-DAV	יוֹנָדָב
Yonatan	Jonathan	yo-na-TAN	יוֹנָתָן

Hebrew Name	English Name	Pronunciation	Hebrew
Yoram	Joram	yo-RAM	יוֹרָם
Yosef	Joseph	yo-SAYF	יוֹסֵף
Yoshiyahu	Josiah	yo-shi-YA-hu	יֹאשִׁיָּהוּ
Yotam	Jotham	yo-TAM	יוֹתָם
Yotzadak	Jozadak	yo-tza-DAK	יוֹצָדָק
Yozavad	Jozabad	yo-za-VAD	יוֹזָבָד
Zanoach	Zanoah	za-NO-akh	זָנוֹחַ
Zecharya	Zechariah	z'-khar-YAH	זְכַרְיָה
Zerach	Zerah	ZE-rakh	זֶרַח
Zerubavel	Zerubbabel	z'-ru-ba-VEL	זְרֻבָּבֶל
Zevulun	Zebulun	z'-vu-LUN	זְבוּלֻן
Zilpa	Zilpah	zil-PAH	זִלְפָּה
Zimri	Zimri	zim-REE	זִמְרִי

Jewish Holidays

Hebrew Name	English Name	Pronunciation	Hebrew
Chanukah	Hanukkah	kha-nu-KAH	חֲנוּכָּה
Pesach	Passover	PE-sakh	פֶּסַח
Purim	Purim	pu-REEM	פּוּרִים
Rosh Hashana	Jewish New Year	rosh ha-sha-NAH	רֹאשׁ הַשָּׁנָה
Shavuot	Feast of Weeks	sha-vu-OT	שָׁבוּעוֹת
Shemini Atzeret	Eight Day of Assembly	sh'-mee-NEE a-TZE-ret	שְׁמִינִי עֲצֶרֶת
Sukkot	Feast of Tabernacles	su-KOT	סֻכּוֹת
Yom Kippur	Day of Atonement	yom kee-PUR	יוֹם כִּיפּוּר

Biblical Measurements

Hebrew Name	English Name	Pronunciation	Hebrew
Amah	Cubit	a-MAH	אַמָּה
Amot	Cubits	a-MOT	אַמּוֹת
Bat	Bath	bat	בַּת
Batim	Baths	ba-TEEM	בָּתִּים
Beka	half-shekel	BE-ka	בֶּקַע
Chomarim	Homers	kho-ma-REEM	חֳמָרִים
Chomer	Homer	KHO-mer	חֹמֶר
Efah	Ephah	ay-FAH	אֵיפָה
Geira	Gerah	gay-RAH	גֵּרָה

Hebrew Name	English Name	Pronunciation	Hebrew
Gomed	Gomed	GO- med	גֹּמֶד
Hin	Hin	heen	הִין
Kav	kab	kav	קַב
Kesita	kesitah	k'-see-TAH	קְשִׂיטָה
Kikar	talent	ki-KAR	כִּכָּר
Kikarim	talents	ki-ka-RIM	כִּכָּרִים
Kor	kor	kor	כֹּר
Letek	lethech	LE-tek	לֶתֶךְ
Log	Log	log	לֹג
Maneh	Mina	ma-NEH	מָנֶה
Manim	Minas	ma-NEEM	מָנִים
Omer	Omer	O-mer	עֹמֶר
Pim	Pim	peem	פִּים
Se'ah	Seah	say-AH	סְאָה
Se'eem	Seahs	s'-EEM	סְאִים
Shekalim	Shekels	sh'-ka-LEEM	שְׁקָלִים
Shekel	Shekel	SHE-kel	שֶׁקֶל
Tefach	Handbreadth	TE-fakh	טֶפַח
Zeret	Span	ZE-ret	זֶרֶת

Photo Credits

1:7 Eyal Shtark/Shutterstock.com. 3:9 Wikimedia Commons, 4:3 mikhail/ Shutterstock.com, 5:18 MstudioG/Shutterstock.com, 6:23 James Emery, flickr.com, 7:14 Andrew Shiva, Wikimedia Commons, 8:22 Boris Diakovsky/ Shutterstock.com, 9:1 Faina Gurevich/Shutterstock.com, 10:22 Kobi Gideon, Government Press Office (Israel), 11:26 Noam Armonn/Shutterstock.com, 12:11 Courtesy Israel365, 13:22 Noam Armonn/Shutterstock.com, 14:28 Courtesy of Israel365, 15:16 trabantos/Shutterstock.com, 16:4 len4ik/Shutterstock.com, 17:6 len4ik/Shutterstock.com, 18:22 Avi Ohayon, Government Press Office (Israel), 19:12 Mark Neyman, Government Press Office (Israel), 20:22 Ekaterina Lin/Shutterstock.com, 21:31 Guy Zidel/Shutterstock.com, 23:5 Mark Neyman, Government Press Office (Israel), 24:17 Noam Armonn/Shutterstock. com, 25:2 Sergei25/Shutterstock.com, 26:20 ChameleonsEye/Shutterstock. com, 27:6 len4ik/Shutterstock.com, 28:8 Courtesy of Israel365, 29:23 Noam Armonn/Shutterstock.com, 30:8 John Theodor/Shutterstock.com, 31:10 kavram/ Shutterstock.com

Map of Modern-Day Israel and its Neighbors

The following is a map of modern-day Israel and the surrounding countries

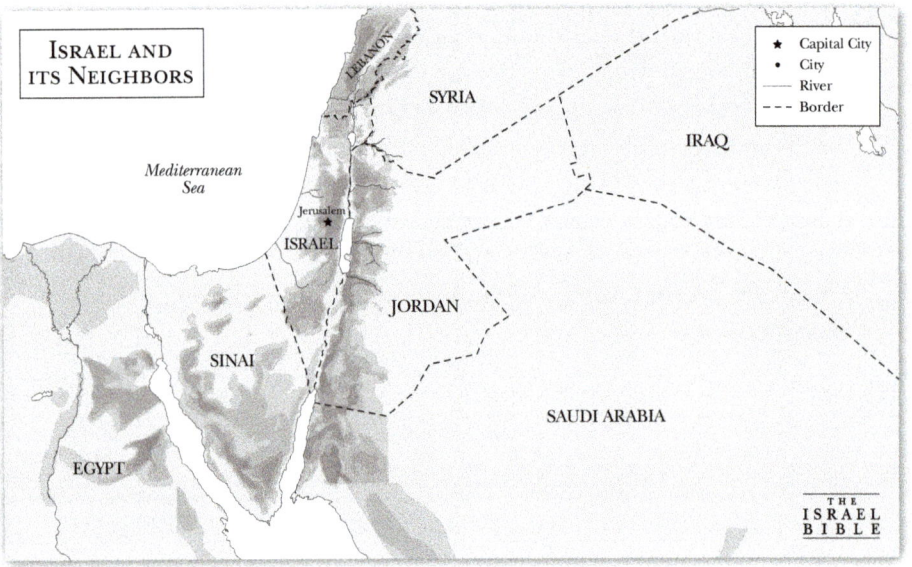

NOTES

NOTES

NOTES

NOTES

NOTES

For more inspiring commentary,
interactive maps, educational videos,
vivid photographs and more,
please visit our website

www.TheIsraelBible.com

THE
ISRAEL
BIBLE